UNDERSTANDING
INVESTING

THE NO NONSENSE LIBRARY

NO NONSENSE CAREER GUIDES

Managing Time
No Nonsense Management
How to Choose a Career
How to Re-enter the Workforce
How to Write a Resume
Power Interviewing
Succeding with Difficult People

NO NONSENSE FINANCIAL GUIDES

How to Use Credit and Credit Cards
Investing in Mutual Funds
Investing in the Stock Market
Investing in Tax Free Bonds
Understanding Investing
Understanding Money Market Funds
Understanding IRAs
Understanding Treasury Bills and Other U.S. Government Securities
Understanding Common Stocks
Understanding Stock Options and Futures Markets
Understanding Social Security
Understanding Insurance
How to Plan and Invest for Your Retirement
Making a Will and Creating Estate Plans
Understanding Condominiums and Co-ops
How to Buy a Home
Understanding Mortgages and Home Equity Loans

NO NONSENSE SUCCESS GUIDES

NO NONSENSE HEALTH GUIDES

NO NONSENSE COOKING GUIDES

NO NONSENSE PARENTING GUIDES

NO NONSENSE CAR GUIDES

NO-NONSENSE FINANCIAL GUIDE

UNDERSTANDING INVESTING

Nina Hill
Certified Financial Planner®

Copyright © 1992 by Longmeadow Press

Published by Longmeadow Press, 201 High Ridge Road, Stamford, CT 06904. All rights reserved. No part of this book may be reproduced or utilized in any form or by any means, electronic or mechanical, including photocopying, recording or by any information storage and retrieval system, without permission in writing from the Publisher.

Cover design by Nancy Sabato

Library of Congress Cataloging-in-Publication Data

Hill, Nina.
    Understanding investing / Nina Hill.
        p.   cm. — (No-nonsense financial guide)
    Includes index.
    ISBN 0-681-41514-2 :
    1. Investments. 2. Finance, Personal. I. Title.
    II. Series.
HG4521.H5715   1992
332.6—dc20   92-9734
                                                 CIP

Printed in the United States of America

First Edition

0 9 8 7 6 5 4 3 2 1

This book is dedicated to my parents,
who always thought I should write about investments,
and to my clients, who inspired me
to do just that.

C o n t e n t s

Contents

Contents

INTRODUCTION

In recent years, investment alternatives and opportunities have increased substantially. Not so long ago, one just went to the local bank (or savings and loan) and deposited funds; savings, these were called. Now there are so many new products that you can invest in such strangely named things as CATS, CARS, and PERCS plus literally thousands of mutual funds and other investment vehicles.

The investment decision-making process used to be easier. With six-month certificates of deposit yielding an extraordinary 16 percent in 1980, an attractive and safe return was easy to obtain. Why look for alternatives? The only question for most investors was for how long they should lock in those high rates.

Today, six-month certificates and money-market funds

yield a lot less, and investors must search for alternatives
that will offer a rate of return that will help their savings
grow. This book is written with the hope that readers will
learn a way to determine which types of investments are
suitable for achieving their objectives.

Real Rate of Return: How much your savings and
investments earn after inflation is taken into account.
For example, if your yield on a money-market fund is
5 percent and the inflation rate is 3 ½ percent, the real
rate of return is 1 ½ percent.

After-Tax Real Rate of Return: How much you earn
after taxes are deducted and adjusted for inflation. If
you earn 5 percent from a money-market fund and
your federal tax rate is 28 percent, your after-tax rate
of return is 3 6/10 percent (0.72 x 5 percent). If inflation
is 3 ½ percent, your after-tax real rate of return is 0.1
percent.

One

WHAT IS INVESTING?

U sually, people have at least two kinds of categories they put their money into: *emergency funds*, money that must remain accessible and *savings*, those funds that can be put away for a longer term objective, such as buying a house, putting the kids through school, or retirement. Since emergency funds should be liquid they should be kept in money-market funds or short-term instruments such as three-month certificates of deposit (available at banks, some credit unions, and savings and loans) or Treasury bills (available at member banks of the Federal Reserve or through brokerage houses). These types of investments fluctuate very little in price and have low transactions costs. Therefore, if you need to get at your emergency funds, you can do so very easily. For more information on these types of investments, see the *No-Nonsense Guide to Money-Market Funds*.

In this book, we will focus on what to do with the long-term oriented savings or investment money.

A rule of thumb for how much to have in your "emergency" account is three-months' wages.

The questions that immediately come to mind are: How long is long term? What are my specific financial goals? How do I feel about taking risks with my money? There are many different types of investments that will answer these questions; some are right for you and some are wrong.

For example, let's say you intend to purchase a house in two years. You have accumulated all but $20,000 for a down payment and believe that you will be able to save almost all of that from your earnings over the next year and a half or so. If so, it would be silly to invest in a developmental drug company's stock, since you may be ready to buy your house before the company has even invented its first drug. A more predictable (safer) investment would be in order. You might wish to invest in a two-year Treasury note that would mature (come due) about the time you figure you'll need the money.

While we'd all prefer to make a lot of money on our investments without taking much of a risk, realistic investment objectives and the disciplined implementation of your plan are the secrets of successful investing. Keep in mind that risk is a fact of life in the investing world. The lower the risk, the lower the expected rate of return on an investment will be. This is because investors require greater compensation—in the form of higher returns—for taking on additional risk in their investment portfolios.

Setting Objectives

Setting your objective is one of the most important decisions you will make as an investor and having an objective will give you something to measure your progress against. If your objective is to earn 8 percent per year before taxes, at the end of the year you can determine whether or not you have achieved your goal. If you have not achieved this rate of return, you should try a different strategy. At least you have control of your objective—which you can't say about the financial markets.

Your objective may be to have a certain amount of money by a specific point in time. If so, you'll need to know how much you can invest and when, as well as how much you believe you'll need at the end of the road. Let's say that you want to buy a house and you expect to need a down payment of $40,000. You'd like to buy in five years and can afford to save $5000 per year. You'll need to find an investment that will give a high enough return to make up the $15,000 difference between the money you'll save and the amount you'll need. Your next step is to determine your required rate of return on your investment in order to meet your goal.

Two kinds of investment objectives are

1. To achieve a specific rate of return
2. To have a specific amount of money accumulated by a certain point in time

---

How to Estimate Your Required Rate of Return

Let's say that you wish to put your new baby through college at a private educational institution. Hospital bills and diapers have depleted your savings, so you have accumulated no funds toward this future financial need, which you expect will be about $175,000 for four years of schooling when your child enters college at age eighteen.

Based on your savings history, you and your spouse believe that you can contribute about $8000 per year to a college education fund. That will still leave you about $31,000 shy of your goal amount of $175,000 eighteen years from now. If you invest $8000 per year, what average return will you need in order to reach your goal?

There's no short and simple way to solve this type of financial problem. (If you wish to solve a problem of this type precisely, invest in a calculator that can compute "present value," "future value," and compound interest.) For our example, we will assume that all of your annual contributions will earn the same return on investment, although it rarely works out that simply. We also have to consider the fact that the money you invest in the first few years will earn more toward your goal of $175,000 than your contributions in the last few years because the longer your money is invested, the greater are the benefits from compound interest.

To approximate what average rate of return will earn the $31,000 difference between what you will save and what you expect to need, start by estimating what you think you will earn on the first year's $8000 contribution. At a compound interest rate of 6.5 percent, $8000 invested for eighteen years will be worth $24,853, for a gain of $16,853. (You can check this on an ordinary hand-held calculator by multiplying $8000 by 1.065 and remultiplying the result by 1.065 seventeen more times.) The second year's $8000 investment compounded at 6.5 percent for seventeen years will return $23,336, a gain of $15,336.

Since the difference between what you are contributing and what you will need is only $31,000, and you now know that the compound interest on the first two years' investments will be more than that, it is clear that your required rate of return is less than 6.5 percent. Therefore, you can afford to put your money into very conservative investments. (An alternative strategy could be to contribute less than $8000 per year to an investment with a higher rate of return—and with more risk—and apply the difference to a different financial goal.)

Narrowing Down the Choices

Now that you know your required rate of return, you can start to narrow down the choices among investments that will fit the bill. Generally speaking, it is best to choose an investment that has a high chance of achieving the minimum required rate of return you have selected. Let's say the required rate of return is 7.5 percent, your time horizon is ten years, and you want the investment with the highest degree of safety. Treasury bonds with a ten-year maturity that have a 7.5 percent yield to maturity (the approximate rate of return over the life of the bond) would be the best choice.

Financial goal setting can help you narrow down the multitude of investment options and help you figure out what might be right for you. By setting goals before you even start to consider different investment alternatives, you can make more rational decisions, have a better chance of choosing an investment with returns that will deliver what you want and, with luck, you will avoid the pitfalls of impulse buying and selling.

Depending on where you are in life, you will have different objectives. Typical financial objectives over one's lifetime are buying a house, putting the kids through school, saving funds for retirement, providing for sufficient income during retirement while preserving capital, and estate planning. Or, you may have different objectives, such as accumulating enough money to go into business for yourself. The important thing is always to bear in mind just what you are investing for—a *future* financial need.

The process of quantifying your objectives by estimating your required rate of return is rational by nature. You want to find the investment with the lowest risk that will offer the rate of return that will fulfill your financial goals. However, when dealing with risk, you also must consider the emotional aspects. No investment is worth losing sleep over. You may find that the level of risk involved in investments that offer higher rates of return is not for you. If so, you will need to invest additional funds at a lower rate of return in order to achieve your goal; or, you may elect to extend the time horizon for achieving that goal (such as retiring at age sixty-five instead of age sixty-three).

Another aspect of investing that is often more emotional than rational is the investment of "found money." Many times, investors will view financial windfalls differently than money diligently saved over the years and so are willing to take bigger risks. If you find that you fall into this category, consider establishing a separate account, since your investment objective for these funds may be substantially different than that for your hard-earned savings.

The Investment Pyramid

Your required rate of return usually is not achieved by a single investment. More likely, you will choose a group of investments that, when averaged together, will deliver the rate of return you are looking for. Most people want their array of investments to be shaped like a pyramid: the most money is kept in the safer investments and smaller amounts in the riskier ones. You can compute your average rate of return by figuring out the percentage of your portfolio that is invested at each rate of return and adding these figures together. For example, if you have 5 percent of your funds invested in high-risk "junk" bonds that yield 12 percent, 40 percent invested in stocks that you expect will return 11 percent, and 55 percent invested in Treasury bonds that yield 7.5 percent, your expected average rate of return will be 9.125 percent ($.05 \times .12 + .4 \times .11 + .55 \times .075$). By combining investments that have varying degrees of safety, you can actually reduce your risk while still achieving the required rate of return. If alternatively, you place all your funds in investments that return 9.125 percent, you'd have all your eggs in one basket—not a good idea. Diversifying a portfolio can keep your returns steady, while lowering your overall risk.

Your investment style also should reflect where you are in life. Investments for a child or for yourself while you are young should focus on the longer term vehicles, such as growth stocks or bonds with many years before maturity. As you approach retirement, you should focus more on conservative investments that will produce income with little risk to the principal. After all, at that point you will have less time available to replace the principal if it is lost in a risky investment.

The Investment Pyramid

Commodities
Options
Any illiquid investment
Low-priced stocks
Development-stage stocks
Junk bonds

VERY HIGH RISK

Lower quality bonds (BBB, BBB+)
Earnings turnaround stocks
(companies that are losing money but are expected to recover)
Small capitalization/high-growth stocks

HIGH RISK

Mutual funds specializing in
small capitalization stocks
Medium capitalization stocks
Average-quality bonds (A or AA)

AVERAGE RISK

Asset-backed securities
Unit trusts
Mutual funds (except those specializing in
small capitalization issues)
Federal agency issues
Blue-chip stocks

LOW RISK

AAA bonds and all Treasury securities
Insured bonds and certificates of deposits

VERY LOW RISK

T w o

How to Choose a Broker or Financial Adviser

Okay, you've determined what your financial objective is—be it your first house, retirement funds, or whatever—and you've determined your required rate of return. Now it's time to consider your choices—and to start investing. To invest in securities other than certificates of deposit, money-market funds, and Treasuries, you need to place your orders with an individual who is licensed both by state and federal governmental agencies. But how do you choose the right person to help you invest?

Your dentist might offer you "hot tips" and your neighbor's son works as a bank teller and says he has some leads, but wouldn't *you* prefer professional insights? All "registered representatives"—the official name for stockbrokers, financial consultants, investment executives, or whatever their employers call them—must pass the Series 7 examination before they may buy and sell securities for third parties. Registered reps are licensed professionals, just like accountants, and must scrupulously observe the laws that regulate them.

In this day and age, it is probably at least as important to check out the company your prospective broker works for as it is to check out the individual. Ask if the company carries SIPC insurance to protect your assets if the brokerage fails to meet its financial obligations. Most reputable brokerages carry not only SIPC but they also have supplementary insurance that protects their clients. Ask the brokerage company how much insurance per account it carries for its regular accounts. (Some companies have "deluxe" accounts, which have even greater insurance protection.) It is important to note that SIPC insurance will not guarantee the success of your investments; it only protects you against the failure of the institution where you do business.

Full-Service Versus Discount Brokers

There are two main types of brokers, full-service and discount. If you are a sophisticated investor and know what you are doing at each step of the way, probably you will want to use a discount broker. Discount brokers don't offer advice—in fact, they're not allowed to; they simply execute your buy and sell orders. As a result, the commissions discount brokerages charge are significantly lower than those of a full-service house. Of course, full-service brokerages offer a lot more advice and assistance. They have on-staff research analysts, traders, economists, and other employees who help their customers get information on investments, set up pension plans, estimate education and retirement needs, and they provide advice about how to allocate investments wisely. Also, most full-service brokerages finance literally millions of dollars of inventory of securities and underwrite new issues of stocks and bonds that they offer to their institutional and retail customers.

Questions to Ask
Your Prospective Broker

1. What is the profile of your typical customer?
2. Are there any complaints on file against you?
3. Do you have any customers like me that I could speak to?
4. How often should I expect to hear from you?
5. Will you help me create and monitor my investment objectives?
6. Do you have a specialty?

Questions Your Prospective
Broker Should Ask You

1. What is your net worth? Your income? Your tax situation?
2. What are your investment objectives?
3. How liquid are your assets? (This isn't just to see if you can make an expensive investment. Brokers are required by law to develop a profile of each client to determine investment suitability.)
4. Have you ever invested before? In what?
5. What is your tolerance for risk?

In most cases, the advice a full-service broker offers is developed by the company's research staff and not by the broker—except in rare cases where the brokerage firm allows its brokers to act on their own ideas. A full-service brokerage may also offer more than just advice on stocks, bonds, and mutual finds; many now have sophisticated analytical services available that are targeted to specific financial goals, like retirement planning and college education, that can help you determine what your required rate of return should be.

What Is a Broker Qualified to Do?

Most brokers have more sales experience than investment education, and it is important to be aware of this. But, as investors and investments become more sophisticated, so do brokers, and many brokers are now Certified Financial Planners® as well. CFPs have taken courses in investment, retirement planning, and tax laws, among other subjects, are required to earn a minimum number of continuing education credits, and must sign an ethics statement in order to get their certification.

You may find that your stock or bond broker is also licensed to sell insurance and annuity products. To do so, the broker must pass an insurance licensing examination and must be licensed by the state in which he or she is selling insurance products. In fact, in today's marketplace, you may also find that your insurance agent is licensed to sell mutual funds or that your banker now offers nontraditional banking services like insurance products or money-management services.

The important thing to remember is that you should ask whomever you transact business with what qualifies them to give the advice or the recommendations they offer. There are all levels of competency in the investment business just like in any other profession. All have some basic information to give, but for more sophisticated services like stock and bond analysis, financial planning, and insurance analysis special training is required, and your adviser will have a degree or special certification in those areas.

Your financial adviser may be qualified as a registered rep, CFP, or insurance agent. Additionally, he or she may

Who Is Qualified to Do What?

Registered representative: An employee of a stock exchange member broker/dealer. Can buy or sell on your behalf stocks, bonds, and mutual funds. Authorized to give advice on securities, though usually the advice offered originates in the firm's research department. Typically is compensated by a percentage of the commission revenue generated by transactions.

Certified Financial Planner®: Works with individuals to set financial objectives and coordinate diverse financial needs, such as tax planning, insurance, and investments. Has passed examinations and been certified by the International Board of Standards and Practices for Certified Financial Planners in Denver, Colorado. Is compensated either by fee, or on a commission basis, or both.

Insurance agent: Usually works not only with insurance products (life insurance and annuities) but also with pension plans and other small-business services. Licensed by the state in which he or she passes the exam as well as in each state in which business is transacted. Usually compensated by a percentage of the insurance premium charged or by fees charged for the handling of the pension services.

hold an advanced degree, such as a MBA in finance or a BA in accounting or economics. (A broader educational background will usually result in better advice.) The point is, find out your adviser's qualifications. Interview potential advisers just as you would applicants for a job with MY FINANCES, INC. You may even want to consider asking for a resume or references. Because most brokers are salespeople, they are charming and easy to talk with. But you should demand more than that. The investment busi-

ness is increasingly competitive. Banks, insurance companies, and brokerages are competing for the same client—
you. So it is in your interest to ask for, and demand, the
kind of service and advice you require.

How to Manage a Relationship with Your Broker

Once you have selected a broker who meets your criteria,
make clear to him or her what your needs and goals are.
Sometimes, putting your financial objectives in writing will
help ensure that your broker understands your needs.
After you are comfortable that the lines of communication
are open and working, discuss with your broker how
involved you wish to be in the specifics of the investment
decision-making process. If you have little time to spend
on monitoring your investments or exploring new ideas,
let your broker know that you prefer investments that
do not require constant attention. (If you find yourself
in this camp, you will probably want to take a longer
term approach to investing, rather than a "trading" approach.)

At this time it also is important to discuss which of
you has the final say on investment decisions. Will you
follow your broker's lead, or do you want to have the
full responsibility for the decisions yourself? Another possibility is a give-and-take approach, where you and your
broker jointly decide on investments. Whatever the case,
make it clear up front. A brokerage relationship that
devolves into a "you said"/"I said" argumentative phase
should either be renegotiated or ended. The most important
aspect of your relationship with your broker is trust. If you
don't trust your broker, find one that you are comfortable
with.

Ten Questions to Ask
Your Broker About an Investment

1. What do you expect the return to be in a year's time?
2. How long do you anticipate the holding period to be?
3. How much are the transaction costs (commissions) and when are they charged?
4. What factors will help or hurt this investment?
5. What do you estimate the risk to be in terms of dollars?
6. Why do you think this investment is appropriate for me?
7. Are there any tax advantages or disadvantages to this investment?
8. What is the source of the recommendation for this investment?
9. If I have to sell the investment sooner than the expected holding period, can I, and at what cost?
10. And, most important, ask yourself: How does this investment help my overall investment strategy?

T h r e e

TYPES OF SECURITIES

It seems that every day a new kind of investment is born. This "population explosion" of investment vehicles has been spurred by public demand for new ways to invest and greater ease of investing as well as by the desire by the brokerage community to create new products to sell. An entire book could be written on each of the following types of investments,* but for our purposes, we'll just talk about the basics.

*See the other *No Nonsense Financial Guides*™ for more detailed explanations of stocks, bonds, mutual funds, municipal bonds, etc.

Stocks

There are two main types of stocks—common and preferred. Usually when you think of stocks, you think of
common stocks, which represent equal equity ownership
shares in a company. When you buy stock in a company, you
become a part-owner of that concern and therefore stand to
profit if the company does. You are entitled to vote on
major decisions, like electing officers or issuing more shares
or whether to sell the company to an outside concern.

Stocks are traded on the New York and the American
stock exchanges and the NASDAQ National Market (also
known as the OTC or over-the-counter market). The biggest difference between the exchanges and the OTC market
is that the exchanges are actual physical locations where
traders meet to do business, but the OTC market has no
central location. Most major full-service brokerage houses
have traders who talk to each other by telephone and
computer to exchange shares of stock. Another difference
between the OTC market and the exchanges are their
listing requirements. Stocks listed on the exchanges must
meet higher standards for earnings than OTC stocks and
must maintain a minimum number of outstanding shares
(also called the "float") to qualify for trading. While some
companies whose stocks meet these criteria still elect to
trade over the counter, in general, OTC stocks are issued
by smaller companies, with less of an earnings history and
fewer shares to trade in the marketplace.

In contrast to common stock, a preferred stock does not
represent an ownership interest in a company. Instead, it
actually represents a debt of a company and is reported on
a company's financial statements as a debt obligation.
Usually, an investor buys a preferred stock only for its
dividend yield, since the preferred stock does not share in
the earnings of the company. Preferred stocks are really
more akin to bonds than to common stocks.

A common stock may or may not pay a dividend. When a

company makes money, the board of directors (elected by you, the shareowner) decides what to do with the earnings. These earnings may be retained to fund future business ventures or distributed in the form of dividends, or they may be divided between the two. (This is why young "growth" companies rarely pay much of a dividend—they are retaining their earnings to fund further expansion of their business.) In fact, the main reason to buy a common stock is because you believe the company's earnings will rise and, therefore, the share price of the stock will rise, reflecting the increased value of your ownership interest in the company.

Sometimes, however, the dividend is an important part of the reason to invest. You may have heard the phrase "yield plus growth." This refers to the total return of a common stock investment. A well-rounded portfolio will include both stocks that have high growth potential and stocks that pay a steady dividend.

Total Return of a Common Stock

The total return of a common stock is its price appreciation plus the dividend yield received. For example, if you bought stock in IBM for $100 per share, sold it for $124 per share and received $6.72 in dividend income, your total return would be $24 plus $6.72—$30.72. If this happened over the course of a year, your annual return would be 30.72%. To figure out your net return, add the commissions you paid to your purchase price and subtract them from the sale price.

Common stocks have historically delivered their highest return when they are held for long periods of time. As a matter of fact, the longer you hold on to a common stock, the greater the odds of your realizing a positive return on that investment. Studies have shown that a stock held for one year will result in a positive return about two thirds of the time. If a stock is held for five years, almost nine out of ten times the investor will receive a positive return; if it is held for ten years, about 96 percent of the time the investor will make money. The message here is that stocks are most appropriate for longer term investment horizons. Yet another reason why stocks are best for the long term is that corporate profits—and therefore stock prices—tend to rise with inflation. If one of your investment objectives is to keep pace with inflation in order to preserve your purchasing power (say during retirement), then stocks are for you.

The average return of the Standard & Poor's 500 from 1930 to 1990 was about 9 percent per year (10 percent per year if dividends were reinvested). This is about double the average rate of return from short-term Treasuries over the same period.

Types of Common Stocks

There are several different types of common stocks that you may have heard about. A blue-chip stock is usually issued by a well-known, well-established company that has a large capitalization (high market value in terms of the dollar value of all the outstanding shares). Usually, a company of this type has steady earnings, is well-followed by research analysts on Wall Street, and pays an average dividend yield. An example of a blue-chip company is Proctor and Gamble.

At the other end of the common stock spectrum is a developmental stage stock. This type of stock is generally issued by a company in its infancy that has yet to make a profit from its operations. A developmental stage company almost never pays a dividend because all of its funds are being reinvested in its product or service development. Since it isn't yet known whether the company will be successful in producing and selling its product or service, a developmental stage stock is the riskiest type to own.

In the rather large middle ground between the blue chip and the developmental stage stocks are the small-capitalization (small-cap) stocks and medium-cap stocks, frequently referred to as growth stocks. A growth stock is expected to increase its earnings faster than that of a more established company like a blue chip (and a developmental stage company usually doesn't have *any* earnings).

A special category of common stocks is utility stocks, which most investors buy because of their higher-than-average yields. Although a common stock usually gets most of its total return from price appreciation and only a modest amount of its return from its dividend yield; exactly the opposite is true of utility stocks. Their dividend yield is at least as important a part of their total return as their capital-appreciation potential.

How Prices Are Quoted

You may have heard reference to the bid (or bid side) and the offer (or offering side) price of a stock or bond. The bid is the price you could get if you are the seller of a security. The offer is the price at which a security is offered for sale. If a stock is quoted as "bid at 70, offered at 70 1/4" or "70 to 70 1/4" it means that the buyer pays $70.25 per share and the seller gets $70. The twenty-five-cent difference goes to the trader or market maker of the security, which is how they make their living. In turn, a stockbroker makes a living from the commission or markup that is charged on top of the offering price. For over-the-counter bonds, such as tax-free municipals, usually the broker as well as the trader is paid from the difference between the bid and the offer.

One truism about the financial markets is: Stock prices fluctuate. But what causes stock prices to move up and down, sometimes wildly? Stock market pricing incorporates the expectations of investors about the future of the economy, the earnings of companies, and sometimes even the outcome of political events, such as presidential elections or appointments to important posts like that of the chair of the Federal Reserve Bank. (This incorporation of information into stock prices is usually referred to as "discounting.") For example, when the tragic explosion of the space shuttle occurred, the stock of the company that manufactured the "O" rings traded down sharply within fifteen minutes of the explosion, even though it wasn't until weeks later that this was officially determined to be the source of the problem.

The overall stock market will also trend (tend to go) up or down depending on the expected rates of return that alternative investments offer. During a high-interest-rate environment, the stock market usually suffers, since investors may be able to get high rates of return on their savings with less risky investments. But when interest rates decline, stocks become more appealing because they offer higher rates of return.

Bonds

There are many different types of bonds. The ones that you'll most frequently come across are corporate, municipal, and U.S. Treasury bonds. A corporate bond is issued by a company. Just as a company may raise capital by selling equity (selling common stock), it may raise capital by borrowing the funds. When a company or governmental entity borrows money, it sells bonds. A bond is a debt obligation of the entity, a promise to pay a rate of interest on your money and then return your principal to you at some point in the future. Therefore, it is important to know the creditworthiness of the bond issuer before you lend them money by buying their bonds.

How to Figure Out a Tax-Equivalent Yield

A tax-equivalent yield represents the return you would need to receive from a fully taxable bond in order to net after taxes the same yield you would get from a tax-free bond. For example, if your income-tax rate is 28 percent, and you purchase a tax-free municipal bond that yields 6.5 percent, you would need to find a taxable bond that pays over 9 percent in order to net the same amount after taxes. To compute a tax-equivalent yield, divide the yield of the tax-free bond by one minus your tax bracket. In this example, the computation would be 6.5/ 1-.28 or, simplified, 6.5/.72.

A municipal bond is issued by a municipality—be it a town, state, or other authorized borrowing authority. There are several types of municipal bond obligations, and the main ones are general obligation and revenue bonds. A general obligation bond (GO) usually has the taxing ability of the municipality backing it up. A revenue bond, on the other hand, relies on a smaller pool of funds as its backing—funds that derive from the project the bond was issued to support. For example, if you bought New York Triborough Bridge and Tunnel Authority bonds, the revenues to pay off the bonds' interest and principal payments would come from tolls received by the TBTA.

A GO bond is usually thought of as safer than other kinds of municipal bonds because the source of funds to pay the bond comes from the unlimited taxing ability of the issuer. Sometimes, however, market perception is that the municipality may not be able to raise taxes sufficiently to meet the obligations of the bond issue. This occurred in New York City during its fiscal crisis in the 1970s, and at that time, a new governmental entity, the Municipal Assistance Corporation (MAC) was created to deal with it. MAC received a portion of New York City's local sales-tax revenues and was authorized to raise funds in the securities markets by selling bond issues supported by those revenues. The MAC bonds had a better rating and were better received in the marketplace than the city's GO bonds.

The safety of a revenue bond depends on the source of funds to which it is linked. If the bond's revenue source is a mortgage recording tax (the tax a community charges when real estate is bought and sold) during a soft real estate market, it is then obviously not as good, say, as a bond backed by water or sewer revenues. So in purchasing revenue bonds, the point is to find out where the money will come from to pay your interest and return your principal at maturity.

Bond Ratings—From Highest to Lowest

One question you should always ask when purchasing a bond is its Moody's and/or S&P rating. From the highest (safest) to lowest (riskiest), the ratings are

AAA: Bonds rated AAA (or Aaa) are considered to be of the highest quality and safety.

AA: AA bonds are also very high quality issues. AA and AAA bonds are sometimes called "high-grade" bonds.

A: Bonds rated A have adequate security but may contain elements that represent some credit risk.

BBB: Bonds rated BBB or Baa are deemed investment grade, but are thought of as neither very strong nor very weak. Adverse conditions may significantly affect their credit quality.

BB: Bonds rated BB or lower should be considered speculative investments. Sometimes these are called junk bonds. Unlike most bonds, which are bought primarily for safety and a predictable income stream, speculative-grade bonds typically offer neither.

The only bonds considered to be "investment grade" are those ranked within the top four classifications—BBB or higher. (Fiduciaries such as bank trust companies and pension plans are typically restricted to buying only investment-grade paper.) Unless you are a very sophisticated investor and fully understand the risks of "junk" bonds, you'd be well advised to impose similar restrictions upon yourself.

Bonds are generically called fixed-income investments because the "coupon" rate (or interest rate) of a bond is almost always permanently fixed when it is issued and the rate does not change through the life of the bond. This is an important point, because the cash flow from a bond investment may not buy as much, say, ten years from now as it does today. That's why expectations about the future rate of inflation are so important to the trend of bond prices.

Another common characteristic of bonds is that they have a fixed maturity date (although some bonds also have a "put" feature that allows the investor to tender—return—the bond at a point before the final maturity date). Usually, the longer the time until maturity, the higher the yield on the bond will be. If the credit quality of the bond is good, you'll have a high degree of certainty not only about how much you will earn on your investment but also about when you will get your principal back. High quality bonds have a predictability of returns, which is their greatest appeal as investments.

What Is Yield to Maturity?

Because the coupon on a bond is fixed at the time of its original issue, comparing bonds with different coupons requires calculating their yield to maturity. The yield to maturity (YTM) takes into consideration all the different elements of a bond—its coupon, maturity date, and market price—so that true comparisons can be made. While an exact calculation of YTM requires sophisticated math, a close estimate may be obtained using simple arithmetic. Let's say that a bond has an 8 percent coupon. If purchased at par (one hundred cents on the dollar), its yield to maturity is 8 percent. But what if the bond is selling at a premium or at a discount to par value? These factors must be taken into consideration. Let's say that the bond is offered to you at 102 (102 percent of par); that means you will be paying $10,200 per $10,000 face (maturity) value. Take the interest payments of 8 percent for one year ($800) and divide it by the purchase price ($10,200). The result is 7.84 percent, which is a close estimate of the bond's yield to maturity. If the bond is selling for a discount—say, 97—divide the annual interest payment by $9700, for a YTM of 8.24 percent. You can see that a bond selling at a premium to par will have a lower yield to maturity than its stated coupon, while the reverse is true for a bond selling at a discount.

Bond prices are quoted as a percentage of their par (maturity) value. Usually, par means $1000 per $1000 face value amount of the bond (quoted as either "par" or "100"). If a bond is quoted to you at 98, it means it is being offered or bid at 98 percent of par value, or $980 per $1000 face amount. Likewise, if a bond is quoted at 103, it is trading for $1030 per $1000. A bond quoted below par is called a "discount" bond while one quoted higher than par means that it is trading at a "premium." The reason bonds trade at prices other than par value is because the coupon rate is fixed, yet the level of interest rates in the marketplace changes. So, the way the market equalizes the yield to maturity of bonds is by pricing them higher or lower than par value. If you think about it, this makes good sense. Let's say that you purchased a Treasury bond years ago that has a coupon rate of 12 percent and still has five years left until maturity. A new Treasury bond, also maturing in five years, pays only a 6.25 percent coupon rate. If you sell, you will need to realize a lot more than par value for your 12 percent bond, since it pays so much more than the going rate of interest.

U.S. Government and Agency Bonds

U.S. Treasury bonds are direct obligations of the United States government and are considered the safest of all types of bonds. These issues are rated AAA because they are backed by the "full faith and credit" of the U.S. government. Full faith and credit means that *all* government assets—gold in Fort Knox, national park lands, whatever—back up the bond issue. Treasury issues are called bills, notes, or bonds; the name the issue gets depends on its maturity. Issues with a maturity of one year or less are called bills; two-, five-, and seven-year debt securities (paper) are called notes; ten- and thirty-year issues are called bonds.

Similar to Treasuries are bonds issued by individual government agencies. While not all agency paper is backed by the full faith and credit of the U.S. government, usually it is rated AAA and is considered to be of the highest safety. Some of the most popular agency issues that are backed by the full faith and credit of the U.S. government are Federal Home Loan Bank, Federal National Mortgage Association (Fannie Mae), Federal Farm Credit, Federal Intermediate Credit, and Federal Land Bank bonds.

Which Bonds Have Tax Advantages?

Most municipal bonds are tax-free in the states in which they are issued and are nearly always federal-tax exempt. (Some bonds issued after 1986 may be subject to federal income tax if they are so-called "private use" bonds or if you pay tax at the Alternative Minimum Tax rate.) Treasury bonds are Federally taxable, but usually they are not taxed at the state or local level. Some Federal agency bonds are also not taxed at the state or local level, including issues from the Tennessee Valley Authority, Federal Farm Credit Bureau, Student Loan Marketing Association (Sallie Mae), and the Federal Home Loan Bank.

Zero-Coupon Bonds

There are also many subcategories of bonds, and one of the most popular types is the "zero-coupon" bond. Just as the name implies, a zero-coupon does not have a coupon and does not pay interest semiannually, like most other bonds. Instead, a zero-coupon bond is sold at a discount from its maturity value and the investor makes money by allowing the bond to mature or by selling it at a price higher than that originally paid for the bond. The bond's yield is figured by taking the difference between what you pay and what its maturity value will be and then prorating that amount over the years to maturity. Zero-coupon bonds may be corporate, municipal, or Treasury issues.

It is important to be aware of the fact that even though you do not receive interest payments from the zero-coupon bond, the IRS taxes you as if you have received the imputed interest. For a municipal zero, this is, of course, tax-advantaged just like regular municipal bonds, but for corporate and Treasury zeros, you may find that you have "phantom" income that is taxable, even though you haven't been able to bank it yet.

Zero-coupon bonds are very popular because they make it relatively easy to invest for a long-term need. For example, a parent planning for a child's college education could buy zero-coupon bonds that mature sequentially just in time to pay each year's tuition expenses. For a child entering college, say, in the year 2004, the parent would select bonds with maturities from 2004 through 2007. If today you put about $9400 into a zero that has a yield of 8.5 percent, you would receive $25,000 from the bonds if they are held to maturity twelve years later.

Drawbacks to Bonds

There are, however, drawbacks to some bonds. For example, a "callable bond" can be taken away from you at the issuer's discretion. (This can occur with a preferred stock, which, you may remember, is also a debt security.) Just as you might elect to refinance your mortgage and lower your interest payments when the rates drop, a bond issuer may call a bond when interest rates drop and refinance its debt at a lower interest rate. The call features of a bond are stipulated at the time the bond is issued and do not change over the life of the bond. Therefore, a bond's call price as well as its first call date are very important pieces of information that you will need in determining whether or not the bond is for you. For example, if you are buying a bond to lock in a certain rate of return for over the long haul, a bond with a short time to its first call would not be suitable. Another reason to know a bond's call features is to help you decide what price you are willing to pay for the bond. If a bond is callable, say, at 102.5 percent of par (par being 100 percent of the face value of the bond) and you are being offered the bond at 105, you may not wish to buy that particular issue.

Some bonds also have what is known as an "extraordinary call" feature. Usually, the kind of bond that has this type of call is a housing bond or a dormitory issue. Even though like other bonds this type has stated call features (a specific time before the first call and a stated call price), sometimes the bond will be called at par long before its regular call date. Theoretically, this only happens when the funds raised by the bond issue have not been used up on the housing project, but there have been cases when, during periods of sharp declines in interest rate, issuers of this type of bond have subjected their bondholders to extraordinary calls.

Convertible Bonds and Other Hybrid Securities

There is a kind of security that is convertible—at the investor's option—into shares of common stock in the corporation that issued the bond. The number of shares that the bond can be exchanged for is fixed at the time of its original issue.

Let's say you bought $5000 face value of convertible bonds issued by XYZ Corporation and that the conversion terms are twenty shares of XYZ common stock per $1000 face value. Assume that you paid $4800 for the bonds. This implies that you would be paying a $48 per share price if you were to convert the bonds to one hundred shares of common stock. (We arrive at this by multiplying twenty shares by the five bonds, which equals 100 and dividing that into $4800.) Let's assume that the common stock of XYZ Corp. sells for $40 per share. If you paid $4800 for $5000 face value of the bonds, you paid a 20 percent premium to its conversion price. Normally, a convertible security trades at a "premium" to its conversion price and a 20 percent premium is the normal rate. A higher premium can mean that the bond is expensive relative to its conversion price and a lower premium may mean that the bond is a particularly good buy. So, when considering convertible securities, not only must you take into account the same aspects you do with other bonds—the credit rating, the call features, and the price—but you should also consider what kind of conversion premium you are paying in relation to the price of the underlying security. Because you are always going to be

paying a premium for the privilege of owning a convertible
security (you'll get a higher yield, if that's all you're looking
for, from a regular bond), it is important that you are also
interested in owning shares of the underlying common stock.

Most investors purchase convertible securities because they
offer a combination of growth—like stocks—and income—
like bonds. So it is important to have a positive opinion
about the growth prospects of the company issuing the
bonds, since these will rise and fall in value in sympathy
with the common stock of the company. However, the
advantage of convertible securities is that they tend to fall
less in value when the common stock of the company does.
The trade off, however, is that their value rises more slowly
when the company's stock goes up in price.

A convertible bond is sometimes called a "hybrid" security because it has components that combine aspects of both
debt and equity securities. Similar to convertibles and also
thought of as hybrids is a new class of securities called PERC
stock (preference equity redemption cumulative stock).
Many blue-chip companies have recently issued shares of
this type of security (General Motors, Texas Instruments
and R. J. Reynolds are a few) and, judging by the positive
reaction in the market, more PERC stock will undoubtedly
follow. The concept behind PERC stock is very similar to
what is called a buy-write strategy in stock options except
that it is "packaged" in the form of a security. (The buy-
write strategy will be discussed later in "Stock Options.")

In a nutshell, the holder of a PERC stock receives a
higher dividend than the owner of the common stock issued
by the same company, and in order to earn that higher
yield, the PERC stock owner gives up some of the possible
appreciation of the common stock. In addition, the call
provisions of the PERC stock (stated in the original offering
prospectus) allow the issuer of the security to reacquire it
from the investor at certain prices within a specified period
of time. Also, the PERC stock has a much shorter lifespan
than a convertible bond. Typically, after three years, a
PERC stock will revert back to common stock on a one-for-

one basis if it is selling for less than the final call or "cap" price; or, it will revert on a prorated basis if it is selling for higher than the cap price. For example, the General Motors PERC stocks have a call that begins at $58.92 and declines to $54.08 in two years. If the General Motors common stock is selling for, say, $45 in two years, the PERC stock holder would receive one share of common stock for each share of the PERC stock that was owned. On the other hand, if in two years the General Motors' common stock is selling for $60, it is likely that the PERC stock would be called at the lower price or redeemed for roughly either nine shares of GM common for each ten PERCS owned or the cash equivalent.

Like other hybrid securities, PERC stocks combine the features of both stocks and bonds. The factors that make a stock go up in price—good earnings, a strong economy—will make a PERC stock rise in value, too, though not as much as its cousin common stock. On the other hand, circumstances that cause a stock to go down in price can be good for bond prices. In a slow economy, interest rates decline, which sends bond prices up, so a company's hybrid securities tend to decline less in value than its common stock will in bad times.

Asset-Backed Securities

Asset-backed securities are generally bonds secured by very high quality collateral. The most well-known type of asset-backed security is the GNMA (Ginnie Mae), a federal agency paper backed by the full faith and credit of the United States government. The initials stand for the Government National Mortgage Association, which buys home mortgages from lending institutions and then guarantees them, using the mortgages as collateral for the securities.

A GNMA is sometimes called a "pass-through" certificate because the mortgage interest and principal payments made by the homeowners pass through to the investors who

own the GNMA securities. Obviously, it would be risky if
the return on your GNMA investment depended on the
payments of an individual homeowner, so the mortgages are
pooled to diversify the risk. One GNMA represents payments from literally thousands of mortgages. Each monthly
check you receive returns some of *your* original investment
principal along with the interest due. If you invest directly
in GNMAs, it is a good idea to open a special account and
reinvest that part of your monthly check that represents a
return of a portion of your original principal. (The check
stub will usually specify this.) For many, it is easier to
invest in GNMA mutual funds or unit trusts, which may
allow them to reinvest automatically the principal payments in
additional shares. As you might suspect, the rate at which
your principal is returned depends on how quickly the homeowners repay or refinance their mortgages. If interest rates
drop, people may refinance their mortgages at the lower
rates, resulting in speedier repayment of principal.

Characteristics of a Ginnie Mae

A Ginnie Mae (GNMA) certificate is collateralized by
government-guaranteed mortgages. The attractive-
ness of GNMAs, aside from their AAA rating, is in the
fact that they usually offer a higher rate of interest
than a regular U.S. Treasury bond, and they pay
monthly, rather than semiannually. These payments
represent both interest on and a return of the principal invested. The main disadvantage of GNMAs is
that if interest rates decline, the repayment of your
principal will increase as homeowners refinance their
mortgages at the lower rates. Therefore, a GNMA
investor may receive an earlier-than-expected return
of principal and may have to reinvest at much lower
rates of interest.

Another popular type of asset-backed security is a Collateralized Mortgage Obligation (CMO). In this case, the collateral is not necessarily backed by the full faith and credit of the federal government (though usually it is seen as a moral obligation of the government, like a general obligation municipal bond). CMOs were created mostly to alleviate one of the main disadvantages of GNMAs—the unpredictability of principal repayment. Mortgage payments are separated into tranches (slices) that are short-, intermediate-, or long-term in their expected duration. Investors who wish to have their principal returned rapidly would buy shorter term tranches; those who wish to lock in interest rates for as long as possible would buy the longest tranches available.

As you might expect, the shorter term tranches yield lower rates of interest than the longer term maturities, just as with other fixed-income securities. Usually, a CMO's principal payments flow first to the shorter term maturities, while the longer term maturities get interest only.

As each tranche is paid off in its entirety, the next tranche begins to receive principal payments. Please note that while we have used the word "maturity" here, CMOs do not entirely eliminate the unpredictability of principal repayments. It is never completely certain when you will get your principal back.

Asset-backed securities have two distinguishing features:

1. Dependence on collateral. Remember, an asset-backed security is only as safe as the collateral backing it up.

2. Uncertainty of principal repayments. While terms such as "average life," "expected maturity," and so forth may be freely bandied about, nobody actually knows when you will get your principal back in its entirety.

There are many other types of asset-backed securities, and it seems likely that even more will be invented because there is great demand for high-quality securities that pay on a monthly basis. Retirees or others who live on the income from their investments tend to favor securities of this type. The most well-known asset-backed securities other than GNMAs and CMOs are those backed by receivables from credit card payments and car loans. As with all fixed-income investments, remember that when you lend funds for a stated return and expect repayment of your initial investment at some point in the future, you must keep in mind at all times the creditworthiness of the borrower. While many tests and simulations are prepared before the introduction of a new kind of security, market and economic conditions can adversely affect the quality of the collateral, thereby substantially affecting the safety of these issues.

Unit Trusts

A unit trust is a portfolio of securities, which could consist of bonds, stocks, or even a mixture of both. Brokerage firms create these units for the convenience of their clientele. A unit trust enables an investor to buy into a diversified portfolio for a reasonably small minimum investment, usually about $1000. While in many respects a trust is like a mutual fund, unlike a fund, a unit trust is not a managed portfolio. Typically, once the trust is created, the securities in it do not change.

For example, an investor with $5000 to commit to tax-free bonds who wishes to lock in a fixed rate of return (which is possible with a unit trust, as the securities are not traded in and out of the portfolio) may consider buying into a unit trust of bonds that is entirely tax free in his or her state of residency. A unit trust offers an investor the advantages of diversification—the trust might own twenty or thirty different bond issues—and a low minimum investment, which make it an attractive alternative to purchasing one individual bond for $5000.

Even though a unit trust's portfolio is fixed, it is still important to remember that what the trust owns is a combination of securities. So, if you are considering investing in a unit trust of tax-free bonds, you'd be wise to inquire just which bonds the trust owns, when their call dates or maturity dates will occur, and so forth. And just like an individual bond, a unit trust might sell at a premium or discount to par value. The difference is that a unit trust's par value is the weighted average of all the bonds it owns rather than the market value of any one individual bond.

A unit trust may also be composed of stocks. In fact, investors who cynically believe that no money manager is able to improve on the market rate of return might consider investing in a unit trust comprised of shares of all the stocks in one of the market indices; the performance of this unit would exactly mirror the market index to which it relates. In a case like this, if a security was added or deleted from the market index, the unit trust would alter its portfolio to reflect accurately the new composition of the changed index.

Mutual Funds

Almost every investor has some money invested in a mutual fund. This is an actively, professionally managed portfolio of securities, and it is a simple and convenient way to invest. Your money-market fund is probably a money-market mutual fund, which invests only in short-term fixed-income obligations. Like a unit trust, a mutual fund owns stocks, bonds, or a combination of securities. Technically speaking, a mutual fund is an investment company, which buys and sells securities for its shareholders.

There are two main types of mutual fund investment companies, open end and closed end, and the open end type is what comes to mind for most people when they think of

mutual funds. Open ends have a floating number of outstanding shares (shares may be created or dissolved as
investors buy more shares or liquidate their position in the
company), and these are always redeemed at net asset
value (the sum total of the investment company's assets
divided by the number of outstanding shares). In contrast,
a closed-end investment company trades like a stock on the
exchanges and may or may not trade for net asset value.

Whether it functions as an open end or a closed end, a
mutual fund's performance depends on the ability of who-
ever is managing the assets owned by the fund. So, your
first step when considering such an investment is to look at
the track record of the fund's manager. (You may wish to
compare the fund's performance with the appropriate market index or with that of other, similar funds.) Another
important consideration is how the fund performs in bad as
well as in good markets. Are the returns on the fund highly
volatile from year to year, or does the fund show a steady
gain?

The Securities and Exchange Commission has standard-
ized the way that mutual fund returns are expressed in
advertisements and sales literature, and all returns are
adjusted for the expense (called "load") of buying and/or
redeeming shares of the fund. This makes it easier for you
to compare the performance results of the funds that will
fulfill your investment objectives. While it is always important to keep the cost of doing business in mind, no-load
mutual funds with lousy performance numbers are no
bargain. First find the funds that meet your financial goals
and then pick the one with the best returns after expenses.

There are as many mutual funds available for investors
to choose from as there are stocks listed on the
exchanges.

After examining a fund's track record (most business mag-
azines have special issues devoted to mutual funds; or, you

might go to the library and look up the Lipper or Morningstar ratings), call the fund and request a prospectus. If you work with a full-service brokerage house, your broker can send you the prospectuses for most of the major mutual funds. Every mutual fund prospectus contains a description of the fund's objectives—it is very important that you read this. If the fund's investment objectives are inconsistent with your own, no matter how good the performance of the fund has been, it is inappropriate for you. For example, if you are seeking income and the fund's stated objective is to produce capital gains, with income only a secondary consideration, you would be wise to pass on that particular fund.

In each prospectus is a section, sometimes called "special considerations," that describes the particular risks of the fund. For example, in the prospectus of an income-producing fund, this section would detail the allowable credit quality of the bonds that the portfolio manager may purchase for the fund.

While, of course, the most important statistic in a prospectus is the performance or net return of the fund (net after commission, internal charges and so forth), you also may wish to examine the expense ratios and turnover statistics of the fund. There is a wealth of information contained in those little numbers on the first few pages of the prospectus: You'll find out how often the manager rotates the portfolio and how expensive the manager's trading strategy is. Usually, a mutual fund that invests primarily in international securities will have a higher expense ratio than a predominantly domestic fund because administrative costs are higher. Also, a mutual fund based in stocks usually has a higher expense ratio than one mostly in bonds.

Finally, you should also look over the sections in the prospectus that relate to the purchase and redemption of shares in the fund. These sections will tell you about when and about how much, you will be charged to buy, sell, or exchange the shares of one fund for those of another within the "family" of funds. (More often than not, a mutual fund distributor will have several funds within the same family or group.) You may also find that you are entitled to volume discounts if you invest a certain minimum amount in any combination of the funds within a family and that you may exchange one fund for another for free, or for a nominal charge.

Major Types of Mutual Funds and What They Provide

Money-market funds: Current income, preservation of capital and liquidity.

Income funds: High level of current income, usually from fixed-income securities such as government bonds, GNMA and CMO securities, corporate bonds, and preferred stocks.

Growth funds: Long-term capital appreciation from investment in common stocks.

Convertible funds: Growth and income deriving from convertible securities.

Growth and income funds: Usually equally weighted for both growth and income. These funds invest in stocks and bonds in varying proportions, depending on market conditions.

International funds: Invest in international stocks, sometimes bonds. Sometimes these specialize in a certain geographic region or industry group, such as health care.

Options

Options are perhaps the most confusing of all investments. At times, they are the most risky, although options may be used either to increase or decrease risk in a portfolio of securities. The kinds of options with which you are most likely familiar are those on stocks. (Options also exist on commodity contracts, but these options are only for the very sophisticated and wealthy investor.)

Stock options fall into two classes. Call options, which offer the owner of the option the right to purchase a common stock for a stated price for a stated amount of time; and put options, which offer the owner the right to sell a stock for a stated price for a stated amount of time. For example, a call option on IBM stock might offer the owner the right to buy the stock at $100 per share until the third Friday in April. Options always expire on the third Friday of the expiration month. (Technically, it is the third Saturday of the month, but who does business on Saturday?)

Components of a Stock Option Contract

Underlying security: The stock to which the option relates

Strike (or exercise) Price: The price at which the option owner may buy or sell the underlying security

Expiration date: The third Friday of the month in which the option expires and becomes worthless

Market price (premium): The price at which the option trades

The aspect of options that most investors find confusing is that you may buy or sell an option to buy or sell. In other words, you can sell an option to buy or buy an option to sell a security. For example, suppose you are the owner of IBM common stock and have realized a healthy gain from that stock. However, you fear that the stock may decline in price over the short term. Rather than selling your shares in

IBM, alternatively you may choose to purchase a put option—an option to sell—for an amount close to the current prevailing market price for the stock. In effect, you are buying insurance against a price decline in IBM shares over a certain period of time (until the option expires). If the IBM actually does decline, your put option will increase in value because the right to sell the stock at a higher price becomes worth more. You may decide to exercise your option and sell your IBM shares at the strike price or, instead, you may decide to "reimburse" yourself by taking a profit on the put option itself by selling it. On the other hand, if the stock does not decline or if it rises in price, you will lose the premium you paid for the put option. This is similar to an insurance policy you might take out on your house. If the disaster you have insured against does not occur, then the premium you have paid to protect yourself is lost.

On the other hand, let's say you'd like to buy IBM stock at its current price, but you are waiting for a bonus check from your employer, which you won't receive for a few months. What you might consider doing is purchasing a call option, which offers the right to buy the stock at a stated price for a certain period of time. So even if IBM rises substantially in price, your call option has locked in a purchase price—you need only pay the exercise price of the option when you are ready to buy the common stock.

The purpose of using stock options as just described is to reduce or control price risk in a portfolio; sometimes these methods are called "hedging." The other main way that options are used to control risk is by using a "buy-write" or a "covered write" strategy. The difference between the two is that in a buy-write the investor implements the strategy when the stock is first purchased. In a covered write, the strategy is implemented with a stock that is already owned by the investor. In either case, the concept is the same.

"Writing" covered calls means that you are selling to someone else the right to purchase a security that you own;

again, this arrangement is for a stated price and for a stated period of time. In this case, you receive, rather than pay, the premium (the market price) for the option. Many investors use this strategy to increase the income of their portfolio. Of course, you must be prepared to let your stock go at the strike price should the option be exercised against you. The alternative to letting the stock go is to buy back the option you have sold. (This is called being "short" the option.) Most likely, you would be buying back the option at a higher price, meaning you would take a loss. If, on the other hand, the price of the stock declines, you may wish to buy back the option because you could do so at a lower price than that which you sold it for. In this strategy, the best of all possible worlds occurs when the stock stays right below the exercise price of the option until its expiration date. This means that the option you have sold will expire worthless and you not only get to keep the option premium you have taken in, but you also still own the stock. Frequently, investors pursuing this strategy will "roll out" to a new expiration month—meaning, they take in a new premium by selling another option with a new expiration date, farther in the future.

So far we've talked about conservative options strategies. But options may also be used as a gamble: to try for a high return on low stakes. These strategies are suitable only for very sophisticated investors, so we will only touch briefly on them. Some investors who have a strong opinion on a stock or on the market may wish to bet on the market by purchasing call or put options. If you think a stock or the market will go up in price, you buy a call option. If you think it will go down, your bet is placed using a put option. Because options are innately leveraged (you might be able to control a hundred shares of IBM for a few hundred dollars), big gains and losses can result from options trading. If you are speculating on the market by trading options, you should consider it betting, not investing. Be prepared to lose your entire stake.

Selling an option short—selling an option by borrowing it from someone else with the hopes of purchasing it at a lower price in the future —entails even more risk. When you sell anything before you own it, you can lose more than your original stake. Brokerages are required by law to get even more detailed financial information about you than usual to assess whether your taking such a risk is appropriate and to inform you, through risk-disclosure statements, how many different ways you can lose your money. If you pursue options strategies of any kind, read the disclosure material your broker will send to you. It is in your best interest to understand all the risks involved.

Seasoned options traders have said that, on average, they lose on eight out of ten trades. That means their gain on the two winning trades must be large enough to offset the losses on the others. When you are trading, try to "fold" or terminate a losing position quickly, and let your winners run.

Warrants

A warrant is like an option in that it gives its owner the right to purchase shares of common stock for a stated price for a stated period of time. Unlike options, however, warrants' expiration dates may be several years rather than several months in the future. Sometimes warrants are sold attached to common stock and are called "units." At some point in time, these units may be split into their component parts of common stock and warrants. Many small companies utilize warrants to encourage investors to buy their stock—sort of like food companies that create coupons for customers to bring to the store.

Real Estate Investment Trusts

A real estate investment trust (REIT) is a special type of business organization that issues shares which are traded like stocks on the exchanges. A REIT owns real estate assets comprised either of the equity (property), the debt (mortgages), or both. In order to qualify as a REIT, 90 percent of the trust company's income must be derived from rents, interest, gains, and from other areas related to its real estate activities.

REITs usually have a higher-than-average dividend yield. In addition, the dividends may have a tax-deferred component, which allows you to delay paying taxes on part or all of the income derived until you sell your shares. Another advantage to REITs is that many trade on the exchanges at a significant discount compared to the value of the real estate they own. If you are considering an investment of this type, find out how much the real estate has been appraised for and how well the company is covering the dividend distribution (that is, if the company's cash flow per share is higher than the amount of dividend paid per share). If the company is financially strong and owns real estate valued substantially higher than its shares, a REIT can be an interesting long-term investment for income and for growth. Because REITs are real estate investments, however, their performance may suffer during downturns in real estate markets, especially during periods of high interest rates or economic recession.

Master Limited Partnerships

Master limited partnerships (MLPs) are another type of security that trades like a stock on the exchanges but, in this case, the business is organized as a partnership rather than as a corporation. Investors in shares of MLPs are limited partners, and the sponsor of the shares is typically

the general partner (or partners). Many of these partnerships are involved in businesses relating to natural re-
sources, such as oil and gas production, or transportation,
logging, or real estate.

The tax-reporting requirements for owners of securities
of this type are somewhat tedious and require filing special
forms. On the plus side, however, MLPs frequently offer
very high yields and the opportunity to realize substantial
capital gains if the businesses are profitable.

F o u r

TYPES OF INVESTMENT
ANALYSIS

Now that you have an idea of what kinds of investments are out there and which are most likely to be appropriate for your needs, it is time to do a bit of fine-tuning. Let's say that, based on your personal financial objectives, you've decided that stocks are the most suitable investment for you. How do you go about deciding which stock or stocks to buy?

Professional money managers and investment analysts may use one or several valuation methods in combination to come up with their final stock selections. No matter what the method of analysis, the goal is to determine whether a stock is undervalued, overvalued, or fairly valued by the marketplace. Rational investors wish to purchase shares that are undervalued in the hope that the market will eventually place a higher price on the securities. In contrast, investors should sell to take profits in or avoid stocks that are overvalued by the marketplace.

Fundamental Analysis

The most widely used method of determining a stock's theoretical value is called fundamental security analysis. (This is also called Graham and Dodd analysis, named for the individuals who popularized the method.) Fundamental analysis looks at a company's balance sheet, its cash flow, the earnings per share, the book value of its stock, and its dividends. The company's management may be interviewed as well and data about new product development and marketing efforts may also be factored into the analysis. By gathering and analyzing this type of data, the analyst comes up with a theoretical price for the shares of the company.

Thus, fundamental analysis attempts to determine the ability of a company to earn higher profits (earnings per share), which are assumed to relate intrinsically to the current and future price of the company's stock. The greater the potential for ever-higher earnings, the more likely it is that a fundamental analyst will recommend purchase of the security. On the other hand, a particular company's business may currently be good, but if an analyst believes that for some reason its earnings will decline in the future, he or she will probably rate its stock as a "hold" or even recommend it as a "sell." In general, fundamental analysis is best used to determine whether a stock is a good long-term investment (as opposed to a short-term trade) because it examines the trends that will develop over time.

While most fundamental analysts have advanced educational credentials (like a masters in business administration or an accounting degree) or professional credentials (like Chartered Financial Analyst certification), you may want to look at some of the same data the pros do when considering a security for purchase. Get your hands on the company's latest annual and quarterly reports; these are sometimes called "10K" and "10Q" forms. All publicly traded companies are required to provide detailed financial information about themselves, and if you call the investor relations or the corporate communications department at the company you are interested in, usually they will be happy to provide you with any information you request.

Financial Information to Look for in an Annual Report

These are some basic things to look for when reading an annual report.

Book value per share: This is an accounting number that assigns a value to the company's tangible assets. Divide this figure by the number of the company's outstanding shares (which is included also in the financial information in the annual report) and compare this to the price of the security in the marketplace. If the stock trades close to or below book value, it could be undervalued and may be a real bargain.

Earnings per share: The company's total earnings divided by the number of its common shares outstanding represent its earnings per share. Look not only for good earnings in the most recent quarter but also at the trend of earnings. Are they increasing or decreasing? Note that "fully diluted" earnings take into consideration the number of common shares in relation to the number of convertible bonds or preferreds and the potential exercise of warrants (which could add to the number of common shares outstanding).

Cash flow per share: This is a measure of the net amount of money received by the company from its operations divided by the number of outstanding shares. Cash flow is the difference between "sources of cash" and "uses of cash." When a company sells an asset, it is a source of cash. When it buys an asset (or pays its employees, for example), it is a use of cash. More money coming in than money going out is a positive cash flow, which can be a very good measure of a company's profitability because it excludes factors such as noncash charges like amortization and depreciation (which are funds "used," but only for tax purposes).

Dividend yield: This is the amount of the annual dividend per share paid by the company divided by the price of the common stock. Look not only at the amount but also at the rate of increase of the dividend over the years. If a company has a history of regularly increasing its dividends, an investor looking for income that is likely to rise with the rate of inflation may find the company particularly interesting. However, if a company pays no dividend, look more closely at its earnings per share and at the funds it is devoting to research and development. If the company is making money and is reinvesting its earnings to expand the business, you could make up in increased capital appreciation on the stock what you forgo in current income from dividends. An investor who wants long-term growth would find this company more interesting than an investor looking for current income.

Current ratio: This is a measure of the short-term liquidity of a corporation. It represents the amount of money a corporation has available divided by the monthly expenses it needs to meet. The higher the current ratio, the more cash a company has on hand. (Most blue-chip companies have a current ratio in excess of 1.2 to 1.) A high current ratio usually means the management of the company is conservative in managing its balance sheet.

Along with hard financial data, most annual reports contain a message from the president or the top executive of the corporation that explains the previous year's results and expectations and plans for the future. This will give you an idea of how the company sees itself strategically. In addition, an annual report may also include separate sections detailing the performance of each operating subsidiary or subgroup. There may also be charts and graphs depicting the trends of the company's stock price or earnings growth over time. All of this is provided to inform you, the investor or shareowner, about the results of the company's operations.

Remember, though, that an annual report also serves as a public-relations tool for the corporation. Sometimes it is necessary to dig into the financial information and the footnotes to that information to get a true and complete picture of what is going on at the company. That's one reason why many fundamental analysts insist on visiting the company and speaking personally with management and employees. As an individual investor, you probably can't do that. You can, however, call the investor relations person who sent you the annual report and ask further questions.

Other sources of information that fundamental analysts use include: Standard & Poor's and Dun and Bradstreet corporate reports (available at most libraries), newspapers (such as the *Wall Street Journal*) and other business periodicals that report and comment on corporate earnings, and the Securities and Exchange Commission (which keeps track of sales of stock and corporate insider purchases—when a company's managers spend their own money to buy stock in the company, it's usually a good sign).

Technical Analysis

Unlike fundamental analysis, which looks at the performance of a company, technical analysis isolates and analyzes the performance of a company's security in the marketplace. Some technicians, or "elves" as they sometimes are called, justify using this method by pointing to the "efficient markets theory." This theory states that the market instantaneously and fully incorporates all available information and assumes that, therefore, stock prices in and of themselves include all the information available on a company. If, indeed, a stock's price does include all the information available, then the study of a stock's price movements alone should be the most effective method of analysis.

* * *

Therefore, technical analysis examines the patterns of stock price fluctuations. It evaluates both price and volume patterns in stocks by using charts of prices and trading volume as well as other market statistics. Because technical analysis focuses exclusively on these numbers, it is more short term in its orientation and, therefore, is frequently utilized by those who seek to time the market for stock trading or who have short expected holding periods.

Stock price charts are the main reference source for market technicians, and they may be obtained by subscription through Standard & Poor's or William O'Neal & Co. Since charts are very expensive (costing hundreds of dollars per year), if you are interested in technical analysis, try a trial subscription (which can be had for a more reasonable sum).

Frequently Used Terms in Technical Analysis

Advance-decline ratio: The number of advancing issues in the market divided by the number of declining issues, usually averaged over a period of days or weeks. When the ratio exceeds 1.6, the market can be considered "overbought" or near a short-term peak. A ratio below 0.6 indicates that the market is near a low point.

Breakout: A rise in a security's or an index's price above a previous high or a drop below a previous low. Usually believed to indicate a continuation of a move in whatever direction the breakout occurs.

Support level: The price at which a security has bottomed out in the past. "Testing support" means that the security is approaching the previous low, but if the support is "held," and the stock does not make a new low, then usually the security rallies significantly. Breaking down below support, however, is a bearish sign.

Resistance: The price at which a security usually stops going up frequently just below a previous high (also called "overhead supply"). If a stock breaks out above its resistance, it is a very bullish sign.

Gap: The area on a chart where there is a discontinuity in price. For example, if a stock closes one day at $95 and opens the next at $98, the space between 95 and 98 is called the gap. When a stock retraces the space between (in this case, between 95 and 98) it is "filling the gap."

Technical analysts use stock charts and market data such as short interest (the total of the number of shares sold short) and mutual fund cash levels to form their conclusions about the direction of stock prices. Sometimes, technical analysts also consider factors that are harder to quantify, such as market sentiment (how many investors are optimistic or pessimistic about future prospects). To an extent, technical analysis depends more on the skill of the interpreter of the data than on the data itself. It is difficult to imagine two fundamental analysts disagreeing substantially about the interpretation of downward trending earnings. However, it is more common for technicians to disagree about the proper interpretation of, say, a pattern on a stock chart. Part of the reason for this is that technical analysis is short-term in its application. Two stock traders could analyze a stock similarly, but one looking for a gain of ten points over the next six months might rate it a lousy buy, while the other, looking for a gain of two points in the next week or two, might consider it a great buy.

In any event, just knowing at what price a stock has been trading in the recent past is an interesting piece of information to have. For example, if you know that the price of a stock you are interested in purchasing has risen by 5 percent in three days, you may want to inquire about why this has occurred.

Quantitative Analysis

Somewhere between the systems of technical analysis and fundamental analysis lies quantitative analysis. "Quants" use data that cover not only earnings, cash flow, and other company-specific fundamental factors, but also look at data encompassing the historical price performances of certain stocks and industries. Usually, a quantitative analyst will also factor in broader fundamental data—for example, that relating to the level of interest rates or the state of the economy.

Typically, a quantitative analyst attempts to predict the overall market rather than the trends of individual securities. Market allocation models, which recommend the proportion of your investments that should be in stocks, bonds, or cash, are usually based on quantitative analysis.

Stock prices are already adjusted for the future value of the company's earnings. The stock market discounts the future by weeks, months, or even years. Therefore, investors should make their decisions on the basis of what they expect to happen, not what has already happened.

F i v e

INVESTING STRATEGIES
AND STYLES

Now that you've decided what you are trying to accomplish by investing, what kind of broker you are comfortable working with, what information you will need your broker to provide to you, what kinds of securities will most likely help you accomplish your financial goals, and you understand how those securities are evaluated by the professional, you are ready to start constructing an investment portfolio. What follows is a look at some of the popular strategies that are used to develop investment portfolios.

Diversification

A diversified portfolio enables you to spread your risks and it will help you reduce the likelihood of making a major investment mistake. Usually a portfolio is not only diversified within an investment classification but also among types of investments. For example, most investors prefer to own a combination of stocks and bonds rather than just one or the other. This helps stabilize the performance of a portfolio because there are times when bond performance can improve the return of a portfolio (like during a bear market in stocks).

You may, however, choose to invest only in stocks. To diversify a stock portfolio of any size, you will need about ten different securities in unrelated industries. (This "rule" can be proven statistically.) More than ten does not significantly further reduce market risk; fewer than ten will not adequately spread the risk. It is important to remember that the securities should not be related (for example, computer and semiconductor stocks are related) or you will not achieve the diversification you need.

To diversify a bond portfolio, choose bonds from many different issues and, preferably, in unrelated industries. If your bond portfolio is composed of tax-free bonds and you are uncomfortable about the financial condition of the state where you live, consider diversifying your portfolio among many geographic regions of the country. You may give up some tax advantages, but you will gain additional safety. It is also advisable to select a mixture of general obligation and revenue bonds for a tax-free bond portfolio.

A fully diversified portfolio might contain stocks, bonds, mutual funds, and perhaps even other types of investments, such as real estate or gold coins.

Dollar-Cost Averaging

Dollar-cost averaging involves the regular, periodic investment of equal dollar amounts in the same securities. Because this investing strategy does not involve an attempt to
predict or time the market, the securities are usually
acquired over a wide range of price levels, with more shares
being purchased in the lower price range and fewer in the
higher. Frequently this strategy is used when purchasing
shares of mutual funds or other longer term investments.

Trend Following

Perhaps the most well-known trend-following system is the
one developed by the Value Line Investment Survey. The
concept behind this system is that companies that have
good records of producing consistent earnings are likely to
continue to do so. In other words, the Value Line method
implies that you will buy high with the intent of selling even
higher. (Stocks that are widely known as having the ability
to produce good financial results are not going to be offered
for sale at the low price of the year.)

The Value Line method is a fundamental trend-following
system; that is, it follows earnings trends. On the other
hand, a technical trend-following system follows the price
trends of a stock or a market index. The notion here is that
a price trend will persist until it is reversed.

"Don't fight the tape" is an expression used in a
technical trend-following system. The trend follower
will tell you that if the trend of a security is up, don't
bet it will decline. By the same token, if a security has
been trending lower, it is believed that it will usually
continue to drop in value.

Contrary Analysis

A contrarian likes the opposite of what a trend follower might. The notion is, if things can't get better, they only can get worse; or, if things can't get worse, they've got to get better. So, it is in the nature of a contrary investor to buy on the worst conceivable news and to sell when everyone else agrees that the news just couldn't be more wonderful.

While a trend-follower will generally favor stocks trading at or near their highest prices, a contrarian attempts to pick stocks for purchase at or near their lows. Unfortunately, cheap stocks have been known to get a lot cheaper, so investors using this method are advised to be very disciplined and to establish ahead of time what amount of money they are willing to risk. Attempting to pick tops and bottoms in individual stocks or in the overall market—which is what a contrarian tries to do—is riskier (and much harder) than participating in an existing trend.

Some of the signals a contrarian might look for in selecting stocks for purchase, or in timing the market in general, include clusters of extremely negative magazine and newspaper articles (particularly in publications such as *Business Week*, *Barron's*, and *The Wall Street Journal*, which are geared to the investment community), management changes that could denote a shift in a company's business tactics, and climactic events (like the suicide of a major executive). For example, a *Business Week* front cover showing a bull (as in a bull market) with steam pouring forth from its nostrils, looking as if it is ready to charge ahead, would be interpreted by a contrarian as a major signal to sell.

"Buying straw hats in December" is the approach taken by a contrarian.

Value Analysis

Perhaps value analysis is the investing strategy that requires the greatest patience—although it frequently offers the greatest rewards over the long run. In using this style of stock selection, the value investor looks for companies that are out of favor or have been overlooked by the investing public. While a contrarian looks for stocks the public despises, a value investor looks for stocks that, for whatever reason, simply have little interest for most investors.

Stocks selected by value-oriented investors usually have in common low price-to-earnings ratios (usually less than 10 to 1), low price-to-book value (less than 1.2 to 1), and a lack of institutional research coverage. Frequently, an undervalued company also has what might be termed "hidden" assets, which give its stock a greater value than is reflected in the price the marketplace assigns to it. Of course, if these factors were widely known and remarked upon by those whose business it is to keep track of such things, the stock would not fall under the domain of a value investor. So, a value investor buys this undervalued stock and then waits for the rest of the investing public to wise up to just how valuable the company really is. The average holding period for the stocks selected by using this method is much longer than is usual (figure on a five-year holding period), so this method is not appropriate for those looking for quick gains.

Asset Allocation

Frequently, analysts are quoted in the newspapers as favoring a certain mix of stocks, bonds, and cash assets. This recommendation will change depending on the forecasts the analyst has regarding trends in levels of interest rates, corporate earnings, and so forth. This asset mix is called an "asset allocation model." The presumption is that investors should alter their portfolios, regardless of their individual goals and objectives, to reflect the current state of affairs in the economy. Of course, on a practical basis one compromises. It makes sense to keep your investment portfolio up-to-date with what's going on in the world, but to do so at the expense of your financial goals would be pointless. Remember, always, the ONLY aspects of the financial markets that you as an investor can control are your personal objectives and how you progress toward accomplishing them.

Indexing

Over the past several years "indexing" has become a popular investing strategy, as many investors—including some very sophisticated ones—have taken the view that no method of analysis will produce returns better than a random selection of stocks. (History frequently proves that these investors have it right!) Studies have shown time and again that most professional money managers, much less individual investors, simply cannot produce results that improve on the market averages. As a result, many investment vehicles have been created that mirror a market index. Mutual funds, unit trusts, options, and other types of investment alternatives exist that are entirely related to the performance of a particular index.

If you are considering this type of investing strategy, be aware that there are a variety of market indices embodying many different types of stocks. For example, the Standard & Poor's 500 index is comprised of the five hundred largest corporations on the exchanges. By contrast, the Wilshire 5000 index reflects the performance not only of a lot more stocks but also lists the securities of many small companies.

Fixed-Income Strategies

Most of the strategies we have been discussing relate to stock investments because fixed-income assets are mostly managed using a "buy and hold" strategy. In other words, when most investors buy bonds, they tend to hold them until they mature or are called away. In fact, until recently, many professional money managers followed the same philosophy. However, in recent years, the volatility of the bond markets has increased substantially; therefore, a buy and hold strategy is not always the best way to manage your fixed-income assets.

There are two basic strategies that you may employ in order to maximize the return of your bonds: matching your maturities to the dates at which you believe you will need the principal; or, altering your maturities, depending on the relative rates of interest being offered at different maturities on the yield curve. Matching your maturities to your expected need for the principal is sometimes called the "immunization" of a bond portfolio. The notion is that an investor may reduce the potential risk of selling bonds in the marketplace by arranging to have the bonds mature at par value rather than accepting whatever the market price of the bonds may be prior to maturity.

The second strategy, which relates to relative interest rates at varying maturities, is somewhat more complex. Let's start with an example. Say that a thirty-year Treasury bond yields 8 percent and that a six-month Treasury bill yields 7.5 percent. The difference between the two yields is .5 percent (fifty basis points, in broker parlance). With such a small spread between the yields at the two different maturities, only an investor with a very long investing time frame and a desire to lock in interest rates would be motivated to purchase the thirty-year bond and take the risk that the security may need to be sold prior to its maturity date (at a price that may either be greater than or less than par value). If, on the other hand, the yield on the six-month bill was 4.5 percent, thereby having a 3.5-point spread with the thirty-year bond, an investor may well desire to extend maturities and buy bonds with later maturity dates, perhaps not as long as thirty years, but perhaps for five or ten years.

The relative yields at different maturities will play a major part in deciding which bonds to buy, hold, or sell. As with most investments, you need to consider the trade-offs between risk and return when making your decisions. In general, if you are interested in fixed-income securities because of the safety that these highly rated issues offer, you're better off focusing on matching maturities to the time line of your investment objectives. On the other hand, if you are interested in maximizing the current returns from your bond portfolio, be sensitive to the changes in the interest-rate yield curve and act according to where you believe the greatest immediate value lies.

The Yield Curve

The yield curve is a graph that shows relative interest rates by plotting the yields of similar bonds (usually Treasuries) whose maturities range from the shortest to the longest times available in the marketplace. A "flat" yield curve indicates that there isn't much difference between short- and long-term rates. A "steep" curve means that there is a great difference between the yields received from short- and long-term maturities. An "inverted" yield curve, which rarely occurs, indicates that short-term interest rates are higher than long-term rates. Usually, a yield curve is inverted only during times of rapid inflation.

Bond Swaps

A bond swap is usually implemented to realize a capital loss for tax purposes, or to improve the portfolio's performance, or both. When you execute a swap, you sell your bonds (usually at a loss) and reinvest the proceeds in different securities. It is important to reinvest in a bond that is substantially different in its issuer, coupon, or maturity, in order for the IRS to allow you to declare a loss for tax purposes. Sometimes a swap will occur to recognize gains (perhaps you had a loss on a stock investment) or to change the character of your portfolio (you may wish to make it longer term, or shorter term, or you may want to diversify your bond holdings into different types of issues).

S i x

PERFORMANCE MONITORING AND MEASURING

As we have repeatedly said: The only aspect of the investment process over which you have any control is your personal investment objectives. Setting objectives will not only help you develop a game plan (which will help you accomplish your goals), but your objectives will also give you something to measure your progress against. Next we will discuss how you can analyze your investment performance.

You should make an annual reassessment of your goals and the progress you have made toward meeting them. Many investors feel that a quarterly analysis is even better, so that any necessary alterations in strategy can be accomplished in a more timely fashion. The easiest way to begin to assess your portfolio's performance is to compare the market-value summaries on your brokerage statements, either month by month, quarter by quarter, or year by year.

How to Read Your Broker's Statement

While not all of your investments may be listed on your broker's statement (for example, the securities in your safety deposit box or deposits you have at your local bank), and there may be some differences among statements from different brokerages (some may give you gain and loss information, some may group asset classes differently, some may show check-writing or charge-card activity), most monthly or quarterly brokerage statements contain the following information:

- The name of the registered owner or owners of the account, the legal address of the account, and tax reporting identification (usually the social security number).

- The total market value of the account (what the account was worth as of the statement date).

- Transactions that occurred during the statement period. These include securities bought, sold, or redeemed; checks or securities that were received or sent out; and dividends or interest credited to the account.

- A listing of the securities held in your account. Usually the statement also shows the market value of those securities. (Note: The market value for bonds that trade over the counter—rather than on the exchanges—is typically estimated and so is not as precise as the market value listed for exchange-traded securities.)

In looking over your broker's statement, start by making sure that your name, address, and social security number are all correct. This may sound a bit overcautious, but a tax audit can result if this information is incorrectly listed on your account. Next, look for the number that indicates what the account is worth. This may either be called "market value" or "account value." Compare this number with the figure from last month's statement. Is it higher or lower? (Unless your broker's statement provides you with gain and loss information, you will definitely need to compare two or more statements to see if you are better off, or worse off, than you were before.)

If the market value of your account has changed, your next step is to determine why. Place the two statements you are comparing side-by-side, and go to the section that lists the individual securities' positions. Go over it line-by-line, and check to see which of the securities changed in price. The sum total of the changes in the prices of the individual securities should equal the change in market value of your account. (Adjust this figure if you have deposited or withdrawn funds from your account or have received dividend or interest income during the statement period.) If you see a change in the value of your account or in an individual security's position that you don't understand or that distresses you, call your broker for an explanation.

Your final step is to look at the transactions section of the statement. *Any* activity in your account should be listed here. (If this is not the case, request an explanation in writing from your broker.) Stock or bond transactions, cash credits, stock splits, withdrawals, and so forth all should be listed in the transactions section of your broker's statement.

How to Translate Dollars and Cents into a Percentage Return

Let's say that at the beginning of whatever time period you are examining, your account was worth $23,500. At the end of the period, it was worth $24,900. Subtract the starting figure from the ending figure (here, the difference is $1,400), and divide the difference by the starting figure. In this example, the account is worth about 5.96 percent more than it was.

Relative Measures of Portfolio Performance

Once you know how much better (or worse) off you are, the next step is to decide how good or bad that is by making a relative measurement of your portfolio's performance. One way to do this is to compare the performance with an objective number. For example, you could base the comparison on a market index or the results from a similarly managed account (like a mutual fund comprised of securities similar to the ones you own). Usually you can find statistics for the quarterly and annual performances of indices, mutual funds, and selected money managers listed in the newspapers. The first issue of the *Wall Street Journal* in January of each year has a special insert listing comprehensive statistics for the previous year's market activity.

If your account increased by 6 percent over the time period in question and the index that most closely mirrors your portfolio increased by only 3 or 4 percent, your relative measure of performance is very good indeed. In 1987, the stock market crash more than offset any gains most investors had achieved during the year, and money managers and investors who achieved any net positive return for that year, even if it was less than one percent, did extremely well on a relative basis.

Another type of relative-performance measure has to do with "opportunity cost." Opportunity cost refers to how well you could have done, had you done otherwise. Most of us are very familiar with this type of thinking about relative performance. How often have you said to yourself (or your broker), "If I had left my money in the bank, I would have been better off." The opportunity cost of an investment is the difference in return between a safe investment and the current yield of a riskier one. For example, if a money market fund is yielding 4.5 percent and the stock you own has a dividend yield of 3 percent, the opportunity cost is 1.5 percent. Usually, though, investors think of opportunity cost as the difference in the return between what they wish they had invested in and what they actually invested in.

Absolute Measures of Portfolio Performance

Most of us, however, are more concerned with the absolute measures of our portfolio's performance; that is, its absolute gains. Your main concerns are making money and achieving your personal financial objectives, not comparing your results to those of the top-rated mutual fund.

By definition, absolute performance is the net return from your investments over the measurement period. If you started with $20,000 and ended with $22,000, your absolute return was 10 percent. If your objective was to earn 8 percent, you have done well, regardless of what others earned on their investments over the same period. Looking at absolute performance is a useful exercise for every investor, but it is only helpful when you have a goal to compare it to.

You may find that your absolute return differs substantially from your financial objective. If your percentage return was a great deal higher than your goal, you may decide to switch to lower risk investments since you may now be able to reach your goal more comfortably. After all, the point is to get to where you wish to go with the least amount of risk necessary. Or, you may decide to continue with these types of investments but contribute fewer dollars to them and allocate the difference to another financial goal.

If your return was lower than what your goal required, you should examine very closely the reasons behind the results you obtained. (A relative performance analysis can be helpful here.) Were you realistic in your expectations? Was your investment thesis flawed (for example, did you believe that interest rates would decline and they didn't)? Did you overestimate the return that a particular class of investments would deliver? The reason could be any or all of these. The important point is that you should analyze why your investments did what they did and use this information to improve your future portfolio performance.

When re-evaluating your portfolio, make a list of what worked and what didn't. Keep it in a file with your other financial papers and review this list the next time you conduct a portfolio review.

Your broker should be willing to help you review your portfolio periodically. In fact, brokers are required to look over your brokerage account at least monthly, so you may find that your broker has helpful suggestions for improving portfolio performance.

Risk-Adjusted Measures of Performance

Risk-adjusted measures of portfolio performance take risk into account. Obviously, the riskier the investment, the greater the expected returns must be in order to entice investors. Your biggest task as an investor is to determine how to balance the levels of risk and return to achieve a portfolio performance that meets your financial objectives but still allows you to sleep at night.

For example, historically the stocks of small growth companies have produced very high returns. But, for any given year, these stocks may be way up OR way down. A stock's price might rise 60 percent one year and drop by 20 percent the next. Its two-year performance still would be quite good (up about 28 percent), but how it was achieved was anything but steady. Price volatility relative to market averages is sometimes referred to as "beta."

So, sophisticated analyses of portfolio performance take risk—the variability of returns—into consideration. Two portfolios may each have returned 10 percent over the same period, but one may have experienced twice the volatility of the market and the other half the volatility. Which one would you rather own? Clearly, the portfolio that experienced half the market volatility would be more desirable, as the risk implicit in it is much lower. In fact, this is the aim of the investing strategies we discussed earlier: reduce the volatility of, and therefore the risk in, an investment portfolio.

How do you determine the beta of your portfolio? Many research reports issued by brokerage firms and by independent analysts such as Standard & Poor's and Value Line will indicate the beta of a particular stock. Many mutual-fund rating services now note the beta of the funds they research as well.

What Is Beta?

Beta is an index of a security's (or a portfolio's) volatility relative to the average volatility of the market. The market overall is deemed to have a beta equal to one. If a security has a beta of two, that means it is twice as volatile as the market is on average. A beta of 0.5 means that the security is half as volatile as the market.

Seven

ADMINISTRATIVE ISSUES

Keeping track of your investments is crucial, not only to keep you on schedule for meeting your financial goals but also to help you in tax planning and, in future years, estate planning. You may find this task as tedious as balancing your checkbook, but it is very important to set aside time each month to keep your financial affairs up-to-date.

Record Keeping

Proper record keeping is imperative. We have already discussed the importance of reviewing your brokerage statements when you receive them. Save these in a file or notebook during the year and then file them permanently with your tax records when you have completed your tax return for the year. A good rule of thumb is to retain your brokerage statements for as long as you retain your tax records. Confirmations of transactions, once reviewed for accuracy upon receipt, may be discarded when you receive the statement that shows the transaction.

You may also find it convenient to record your transactions on a single page: listing descriptions of the securities, how many shares you own of each one, purchase dates and prices, and sale dates and prices. (See Appendix E for a sample record form.) That way, you will have an easy reference for your periodic portfolio reviews and all the information you will need to give your tax accountant at year-end will be completed and ready to go.

Forms of Security Registration

When you purchase a security, normally it is held in "street name" with your broker, which means that the securities are held in the name of your broker, the dividends are paid directly into your brokerage account, and any stock splits or other administrative details will be handled directly by your broker. It also is easier to buy and sell securities in street name; no certificates need to change hands and no additional paperwork is filed. However, if you wish instead to have the certificates issued and sent directly to you, the securities will be "registered" in your name and the issuers of the securities will send you any dividends, additional shares, or information relating to the company.

When you move, let your broker know your new address and phone number. If you "hold your own paper" (have securities registered directly in your name), contact the trust company for each issue and let them know your new address as well.

How Ownership of a Security Can Change Without a Sale Occurring

Regardless of whether you hold your securities in street name or have them registered in your name, the legal ownership of the securities will be the same as the title of the account through which they were purchased. For example, if the account titled is "Mary E. Smith," the securities are registered exactly that way. When opening a brokerage account, signing stock or bond certificates, or doing any other paper work related to your brokerage account, use your full legal name. You should also use the address that represents your legal residence for your account. (The address you put on your federal income tax return is your legal residence.) You may always ask your broker to send your statements to another address or to send a duplicate copy (known as an "interested party" copy) to an address different than the one listed on your account.

Let's say that you have purchased stocks in the name of "Mary E. Smith" and wish to give them to your daughter for tax reasons. To accomplish this, the securities need to be re-registered in your daughter's name. This constitutes a change of ownership (and your tax adviser should be consulted to determine whether a gift-tax return needs to be filed). Because you are changing the legal ownership of the stocks, your broker will have you write a letter asking that the securities be re-registered. Keep a copy of this letter for yourself because the date of the gift could affect your daughter's tax basis for the stock.

Another way—sometimes inadvertently—that the legal ownership of securities changes is when stock or bond certificates are deposited in an account which is titled differently from the name under which the securities are registered. If you have securities that you purchased on your own and then later on you open a joint account with another individual and deposit those securities into the joint account, you are in fact changing the ownership of those securities (and your broker will require a letter from you verifying this). You are effectively gifting one half of the value of those securities to the party who is the joint tenant of the account. Again, double check with your tax adviser as to whether this is a taxable gift, and if a gift-tax return should be filed.

Documents Your Broker May Ask You to Sign

When you open a brokerage account, you may find yourself deluged with paperwork. Remember: *Read everything before you sign it.* Usually a brokerage account requires, at a minimum, that a "customer agreement" or "new account agreement" is signed and returned before the first transaction. This form details your legal obligations as a customer (for example, to adhere to the rules of the exchanges) and will also indicate whether your account is a cash or a margin account. Typically, this form also contains language relating to your rights as an investor, should you have a dispute with your broker. If you intend to trade options, you may be asked to sign additional paperwork indicating that you have been informed of the risks of option transactions.

What is the Difference Between a Cash Account and a Margin Account?

A cash account requires all securities transactions to be paid in full by settlement date (usually five business days after the transaction is made). A margin account allows you to put up only part of the amount of the transaction, initially 50 percent. However, with a margin account you are borrowing money from your broker, and you will be charged interest on the outstanding balance. If you sell the position out, the margin loan must be paid off at that time. *Buying on margin involves significant leverage and therefore adds risk, no matter how safe the investment is on its own.*

If you intend to allow your broker to make investment decisions about your portfolio without consulting you ahead of time, you will be asked to complete a power of attorney or a "discretionary" form. This will enable your broker to buy and sell at his or her discretion on your behalf. While you may cancel trading discretion at any time (send your broker a letter by registered mail if you decide to do this), make absolutely sure you trust the individual to whom you are granting this legal right. Also, you may grant discretion to a party not affiliated with your brokerage firm—your children, for example. Your broker can provide you with the proper forms for this.

There will also be extra paperwork involved if you open an account that includes a trust agreement. Usually the types of accounts that require this agreement are retirement plans, such as IRA and Keogh accounts. Because these accounts must be updated for each change in the tax code, periodically you may need to complete new paperwork for accounts like this. You will also be required to sign extra forms if you have certain kinds of investments, such as limited partnerships or if you enlist the services of a professional money manager.

When the Owner of an Account Dies

When an owner of a securities account passes away, the account is frozen until the administrator or executor of the estate becomes the legal signatory for the assets of the estate. Usually the brokerage firm will require a death certificate, an affidavit of domicile, and a (probate) court document that officially appoints the administrator or executor. When these documents are received, an "estate" account may be opened, the assets of the decedent transferred to the new account, and the executor or administrator is then required to sign brand new account documents (such as the customer agreement). Then the executor or administrator may transact business in a normal fashion, for the benefit of the estate.

E i g h t

PUTTING IT ALL
TOGETHER

The object of intelligent investing is to find a way to achieve your financial goals by taking the least amount of risk possible while still attaining your required rate of return. To help you do this, we've discussed some of the strategies for reducing risk in a portfolio of investments and have noted some of the risks specific to different types of financial instruments. We've also pointed out the need to regularly monitor and assess the performance of your portfolio.

It is important to note that however scientific you may be as an investor, your personal attitudes about money will play an important role in the types of decisions you will make. Since all investing involves a trade off between risk and return, how you deal with risk will affect your satisfaction with the investment decisions you make. If you use a disciplined approach to investing, it is unlikely you will become an investment insomniac, but if you are literally losing sleep over an investment, it is too risky for you and you should look for an alternative strategy. Clearly, there are many combinations of investments out there that will produce the returns you require. By monitoring your investments and keeping track of what works—and what your mistakes have been—you can learn how to become your own best expert.

Whom to Call for Information

For information about a company: The Standard & Poor's corporate report provides a general description of a company's business, earnings, and balance sheet, and lists its phone number as well. For more detailed information, call the company and ask for its "investor relations" or "corporate communications" department. They can answer questions about the company and can provide you with further financial details as well as other information.

For information about a bond rating: Call Moody's Corporate Rating Desk (212) 553–0300 or Standard & Poor's (212) 208–1527.

For administrative (dividend, interest, lost certificates, etc.) information:

For a security registered in your name—call the trust company handling the issue. This information is printed on the face of the certificate. You may also find the trust company's phone number printed on the checks or other correspondence you have received from them.

For a security held in street name with your broker—call your broker.

For questions relating to a called bond or preferred stock:

For a security registered in your name—call the trust company handling the issue.

For a bearer bond—call the trust company.

For a security held in street name—call your broker.

For questions relating to the professional standing of your financial advisor:

For registered representatives—call the North American Securities Administrators Association in Washington, D.C. (202) 737–0900, or your regional Securities and Exchange Commission office.

For Certified Financial Planners®—call the International Board of Standards and Practices for Certified Financial Planners, in Denver, Colorado (303) 830–7543, or the International Association for Financial Planning in Atlanta, Georgia (404) 395–1605.

For insurance agents—call your state insurance department.

For complaints relating to investments or your broker: Call the National Association of Securities Dealers in Washington, D.C. (202) 728–8000.

A p p e n d i x A

INVESTMENT CALENDAR

W hile history does not always repeat itself, especially in the stock and bond markets, there are seasonal events and trends that, more often than not, do recur.

January:

The second best month of the year for capital gains in the stock market.

The "January effect" favors small-capitalization stocks and securities that have been depressed in price due to tax-loss selling.

The second half of the month is characterized by earnings reports for the previous quarter and, in some cases, the previous year.

February:

In the first half of the month, companies that did not report earnings in January report their earnings.

In mid-month the Treasury executes its first quarterly auction of the year.

March:

The first "triple-witching" day (where futures as well as stock options expire) of the year occurs on the third Friday of the month. This is the day when futures contracts on stock indices expire, along with normal options on stocks. This sometimes results in market volatility.

At month-end the first quarter of the year is over. Look for portfolio "window-dressing" by institutional money managers.

Time to review your own portfolio for first-quarter performance.

April:

The market sometimes has an upward bias at the beginning of the new quarter. Look for an up market the first few days of the month.

Companies start reporting earnings for the first quarter.

May:

The second Treasury quarterly refunding occurs around mid-month.

June:

The second triple-witching session of the year occurs on the third Friday of the month. Look for market volatility.

The end of the month also brings the end of the second quarter of the year and institutional portfolio window-dressing.

Time to review your own portfolio for performance for the first half of the year.

July:

The market frequently has an upward bias at the beginning of a quarter. If you are planning to purchase stocks, buy before the Fourth of July.

Earnings for the second quarter start to emerge.

August:

The third Treasury quarterly refunding happens about mid-month.

September:

Triple-witching occurs the third Friday of the month.
    End-of-quarter window-dressing at month's end.
    Time to review your portfolio.

October:

This has historically been the worst month for capital gains in the stock market (witness the crashes of 1929, 1987, 1989).

Third-quarter corporate profits are announced.

November:

Tax-loss selling begins earlier every year. Lately, investors have started their selling in November. This also is a time to look at your own portfolio for tax-sale candidates and for possible bond swaps.

Mid-month, the final Treasury refunding of the year takes place.

December:

The best month of the year for capital gains in the stock market.

The final triple-witching day of the year occurs on the third Friday of the month.

After mid-month, tax selling abates and some stocks that have been pressured by tax-related selling start to rally.

A p p e n d i x B

INVESTING CHECKLIST

Setting Objectives

- Have I established a target required rate of return?

- Have I determined what my financial goal is and the date for its achievement?

- Have I made my objectives clear to my broker or financial advisor?

Investment Selection

- Have I a reasonable probability of achieving my return objectives with this investment?

- Am I familiar with the risks that this security entails?

- Does this investment complement my portfolio by either adding to my expected return or by reducing the risk in my portfolio by hedging the risks of my other investments?

- Do I have an anticipated holding period for this investment?

Investment Monitoring

- Have I set up a record-keeping system to keep track of my investments?

- Have I created a regular schedule for monitoring the success or failure of my investing strategy?

- Have I compared the success of my portfolio's return with what I had hoped to accomplish?

A p p e n d i x   C

CASE STUDY:
HOW TO QUANTIFY AN OBJECTIVE

Mary and Joe Franklin wish to determine how much they need to accumulate for retirement. The couple already has $125,000, which is currently invested in a tax-free municipal bond mutual fund yielding 7.25 percent. Mary does not work outside the home. Joe believes that he will retire from his job as a manager for a major appliance manufacturer in twelve years.

The first step for Mary and Joe is to identify the present value of their expected need for funds at retirement. (We are assuming that they will wish to meet their income needs without touching their principal.) Currently, Joe's annual salary is $65,000. Since Mary and Joe plan to sell their suburban house and move South when Joe retires, they believe that the income they will need will be less than Joe's current salary. After estimating their expenses, they arrive at an annual income figure of $42,000 (in today's dollars). From this figure, they subtract their estimate of what they will receive from social security, about $12,000.

Estimated annual income needed $42,000
Less income from social security . . . . ($12,000)
Funds needed in today's dollars $30,000

Mary and Joe's next step is to figure out how much $30,000 in today's dollars will be in twelve years, when Joe retires. They assume an annual inflation rate of 4 percent. After compounding $30,000 at 4 percent for twelve years, they determine that the income they will need to meet their projected expenses in retirement will be $48,031 (the future value of $30,000 at 4 percent for twelve years).

Mary took her hand-held calculator and multiplied 1.04 (for 4 percent) by $30,000 twelve times (for twelve years) to arrive at $48,031.

Joe's latest statement from the employee benefits department of his company says that he will receive an annual pension of $6,250 when he retires. Mary and Joe subtract this amount from the income they will need from their investments ($48,031 minus $6,250) and conclude that they will need to receive $41,781 a year to meet their expenses at retirement.

How much will Mary and Joe need to accumulate over the next twelve years in order to realize that $41,781 in dividend and interest income from their investments? With interest rates heading lower, Mary decides that a reasonable expectation for returns on their investments is 7 percent. By dividing the amount of income they have estimated they will need from their investment portfolio ($41,781) by 7 percent they arrive at a figure of $596,871. (Divide $41,781 by .07 to arrive at $596,871.) This is the size of the portfolio they need, earning income at 7 percent, to be able to live from their investment income without invading the principal.

Since Mary and Joe have already accumulated $125,000 toward retirement, and they are reinvesting the income from their municipal bond fund (at 7.25 percent), they subtract the expected value of this investment twelve years from now from their target amount of $596,871.

Mary used her calculator to estimate that the $125,000 mutual fund investment would be worth $289,520 in twelve years. She then subtracted that amount from her target amount of $596,871. She concludes that she and Joe need an additional $307,351 to generate the income they expect they will need at retirement.

Since Mary and Joe intend to sell their suburban house and purchase a smaller house when they move to the South after Joe retires, Mary subtracts $125,000 (her estimated difference between the market value of their current home and the price they expect to pay for their retirement home) from the target amount of $307,351. Her conclusion: She and Joe need to accumulate another $182,351 to live comfortably in retirement.

NOTE: Whenever you are estimating a future need for funds, remember that it is just that—an estimate. If inflation runs at a rate higher than the 4 percent that Mary and Joe assumed, they will need to have more money available to invest for retirement. Just as it is a good idea to track the performance of your investment portfolio on a regular basis, it also is a good idea to reassess the assumptions you make when projecting a future financial need.

A p p e n d i x D

SUGGESTED READING LIST

How to Read and Understand the Financial News
Gerald Warfield (New York: Harper & Row, 1988)

The Mathematics of Investing
Michael C. Thomsett (New York: Wiley, 1989)

The Stock Options Manual
Gary L. Gastineau (New York: McGraw-Hill, 1978)

Technical Analysis of Stock Trends
Robert D. Edwards and John Magee (Boston: John Magee, 1962)

Words of Wall Street: 2000 Investment Terms Defined
Allan H. Pessin and Joseph A. Ross (Homewood, Illinois: Dow Jones-Irwin, 1983)

Account Name: _____   Account #: _____

Stock Symbol	Description	PURCHASE				SALE				Gain (Loss)
		Date	Quantity	Price	Cost	Date	Quantity	Price	Proceeds	

GLOSSARY

Account executive: registered representative. Also sometimes called investment executive or financial consultant.

Accrued interest: accumulated interest on a bond from the last (usually semi-annual) payment date. Accrued interest is paid by the purchaser of a bond in the secondary market to the seller of the bond and is recouped by the purchaser on the next interest payment date.

Accumulation area: technical analysis term for the price range within which buyers are accumulating stock. Technicians identify these areas when a stock consistently does not drop below a price zone.

Administrator: person designated by the courts to administer an estate and distribute its assets when no executor is designated in a will.

Alternate Minimum Tax (AMT): Federal tax rate that affects some taxpayers, particularly those with a high amount of "preference items." A flat tax rate that disallows most itemized tax deductions.

Annual report: published by companies to detail and explain the past year's results. Contains financial data and usually commentary from one or more of the company's executives.

Ask: the price at which a security is offered for sale to investors. Sometimes called offer or offering price.

Automatic reinvestment: usually used in the context of mutual funds. Refers to the reinvestment of dividends and capital gains into additional shares. Sometimes used as part of a dollar-cost averaging strategy.

Averaging down (or up): purchasing additional shares at lower (or higher) prices.

Back-end load: redemption fee paid when a security is sold. For mutual funds, sometimes called a contingent deferred sales charge.

Balanced account (or fund): asset allocation strategy using a combination of stocks and bonds.

Basis point: one one-hundredth of one percent (.0001). 100 basis points equals one percent.

Basis price: cost for tax purposes.

Bear: one who is expecting a price decline in the market (or a particular security or class of investment).

Bearer bond: a certificate that bears no registered owner. Also called a "coupon" bond because interest payments are obtained by presenting to a paying agent coupons that are clipped from the bond.

Bear market: a declining market.

Bid: the price a buyer is willing to pay for a security. The price you get when you sell a security.

Blue chip: a high quality investment. Usually refers to common stocks of companies with long records of sustained earnings and dividend payments.

Book-entry: a security that has no physical certificate that can be issued. Records are kept at the Depository

Trust Company and purchases and sales are recorded electronically.

Book value: an accounting number representing the theoretical tangible value of a company. The value at which an asset is carried on the company's balance sheet.

Bull: one who believes the price of the market or a security will increase. A bull market is a rising market.

CATS: Certificates of Accrual on Treasury Securities. A zero coupon bond sold at a deep discount from its maturity value. A CAT pays no interest during its lifetime.

✓ **Certificate of deposit:** debt instrument issued by a bank or savings and loan institution. Usually a CD is federally insured and has a short or intermediate maturity date.

Closed-end (mutual fund): an investment company with a limited number of outstanding shares. May trade higher or lower than its net asset value.

✳ **Common stock:** unit of equity ownership in a corporation. Holders of common stock shares are usually entitled to vote for the corporate officers, attend annual meetings, and share in the profits of the company. Common share owners are subordinated to the owners of bonds and preferred stock as well as other creditors in the event of liquidation of the company's assets.

Conversion premium: the amount by which the convertible security exceeds the price of the common stock. For example, if the conversion price as set out is $25 per share and the price of the common stock is $22 per share, the conversion premium is $3, or 13.64 percent.

Cumulative preferred: preferred stock whereby if dividends are omitted, they accumulate until paid out. Dividends may not be paid on the common stock as long as a preferred dividend obligation is outstanding.

Custodial account: account opened for a minor (as defined by the state of residency) with a custodian as the signatory. Frequently, the custodian is a parent, but does not have to be. By law, custodial accounts must be cash, not margin. When the minor reaches the age of majority he or she may then assume full control of the account and the assets it holds.

Cyclical stock: a common stock that responds to the economic cycle. Automotive, chemical, transportation, paper, and technology companies are considered cyclical. By contrast, stocks in food and drug companies are not considered cyclical.

Day order: an order to buy a security at a specific price that expires at the end of the day unless executed.

Delayed opening: an intentional delay in the trading of a security. Usually occurs when news is emerging regarding the company or when a large influx of orders makes it difficult for an opening price to be established.

Discount: the difference between the market price of a bond and its (higher) face or maturity value.

Discount broker: a registered representative who places buy and sell orders but does not offer advice or other services. Also refers to the company for which the discount broker works.

Discounting: refers to the market's anticipation of future events. A stock will rise or fall depending on expectations of its future prospects.

Distribution area: a technical analysis term for the price range where sellers are letting stock go. Technicians identify these areas when a stock consistently does not rally through a price range.

Dividend: distribution made by a corporation or mutual fund of its earnings. A security's price is reduced by the amount of the distribution on the day it goes "ex-dividend."

Downtick: when a security trades at a price lower than the last previous reported price. Also called a "minus tick."

Efficient markets theory: states that market prices fully and instantly reflect all available information about a company. This theory implies that all securities are fairly valued by the marketplace based on the information available to investors.

Equity: in a brokerage account, it is the market value of the securities (minus the amount borrowed if you are buying on margin).

Estate planning: planning for the minimization of taxes at death and for the orderly disposition of one's assets.

Executor: person designated in a will to administer the estate and to distribute its assets.

Exercise: to use a right stipulated by contract. For example, exercising an option means you are buying or selling the underlying stock at the exercise price stated in the option contract.

Face value: the maturity value of a fixed-income security; also the amount upon which interest payments are calculated. A bond paying an 8 percent coupon with $10,000 face value will pay $800 per year.

Fill: the completion of an order to buy or sell.

Flat: refers to a fixed-income security trading with no accrued interest.

Front-end load: commission charged to purchase a security. Usually used to refer to mutual fund commissions.

Full-service broker: one who provides a wide range of services including research reports, advice on financial planning, access to new stock issues, and offers a large inventory of securities trading over-the-counter on the secondary market.

Good delivery: brokerage term referring to certificates that are presented to settle a trade. If all documents are properly signed and meet all other requirements (for example, a bearer bond requires proof of ownership), they are said to be in good delivery form.

Good-until-cancelled order: open order to buy or sell a security that remains in effect until executed or cancelled. Order may be reduced in price by dividends or other distributions unless specified "do not reduce."

Hedge or hedging: strategy used to reduce risk for an investment or portfolio. Usually involves combining investments that will offset each other under certain conditions. For example, gold, which tends to increase in price during times of high inflation, sometimes is used as a hedge for a bond portfolio that would be negatively affected in price by a rise in inflation.

Holding period: the length of time an investor owns a security.

House call: a call issued by a brokerage firm when a margin account falls below the required level of equity. Usually a margin account is required to maintain at least a 30 percent equity level. If the equity falls below 30 percent, the customer is asked to deposit additional securities or cash to bring the account up to the "maintenance" level.

Index: statistical composite that calculates changes in a collection of data. Indices track price changes in securities as well as changes in economic trends.

Index fund: mutual fund that owns the securities comprising a stock index.

Individual Retirement Account (IRA): personal retirement plan that employed individuals may establish for themselves. Contributions to IRAs are tax-deductible for some individuals. Transactions may be made within an IRA account without recognition of gains or losses for tax purposes, although any transfer of funds out of an IRA account must be accounted for and may result in taxes and/or tax penalties.

Initial public offering (IPO): the first issuance of a security in the marketplace. Brokerage commissions are built into the initial offering price as part of the investment underwriting fees. IPOs are sold by prospectus only. (As with all prospectuses, read it with an eye to understanding the risks of the security.)

Joint tenants with right of survivorship (JTWROS): a form of joint ownership of assets where the assets transfer without probate to the surviving tenant upon the death of the other account holder.

Junk bond: a fixed income security with a speculative investment rating of BB or below from Moody's or Standard & Poor's.

Keogh (HR-10) plan: a pension plan used by unincorporated businesses that allows higher contributions than IRA accounts. Under current tax laws, up to about 13 percent of the net income from the business's activities may be contributed to the plan.

Limit order: order to buy or sell a security for a specific price.

Load: sales charge or commission charge to buy or sell a security.

Long position: owning a security. The opposite of a long position is a short position, where an investor sells a security he or she does not own.

Margin account: brokerage account that allows investors to buy securities on credit with the securities themselves acting as collateral for the loan. Interest is charged by the brokerage firm to the client.

Margin call: request from a brokerage firm that the equity in a margin account be increased. If the equity in the account is not increased, securities may be liquidated in the account to meet the margin call.

Market maker: a dealer or company willing to buy and sell a security at publicly quoted prices, thus guaranteeing a ready market for that security.

Market order: an order for immediate execution to buy or sell securities at the prevailing market price.

Maturity data: the date at which a fixed income security pays out the principal to its owner.

Money-market fund: an open-end mutual fund, usually with no sales load, that invests in very short-term fixed income securities such as commercial paper, bankers' acceptances, government securities, and certificates of deposit. The net asset value rarely changes (from $1.00 per share) due to the low risk of the investments the fund makes. The yield of the fund does change and tracks the yield on the securities in which the fund invests.

Moody's Investor Service: one of the most well-known bond rating agencies (the other is Standard & Poor's).

Moody's also rates other fixed-income securities, such as preferred stock.

New issue: see Initial public offering.

Offer: the price at which a security may be purchased. Also called offering price.

Open-end (mutual fund): an investment company that may issue additional shares at will. An open-end mutual fund is always bid at net asset value.

Open order: limit order to purchase or sell a security good for one day or "good until cancelled."

Option: a contract giving the owner the right to buy (call) or sell (put) an asset at a stated, fixed price for a specified period of time.

Overbought: a term used to describe a market or security that has had a recent sharp increase in price and therefore may be subject to a price decline.

Oversold: a term used to describe a market or security which has had a recent steep decline and is expected to rebound in price.

Over-the-counter (OTC): refers to securities that are not traded on an organized exchange or to the manner in which these securities are traded. Over-the-counter securities are traded by computer and telephone

Par: the nominal or face value of a security. For bonds, a price of 100 cents on the dollar is quoted as par. Par is sometimes used as slang for any security trading at a price of 100.

Phantom income: income subject to income taxation even though it has not yet been physically received by an investor. Taxable zero-coupon bonds produce phantom income.

Point: for stocks, a point is one dollar per share. For bonds, a point refers to one percent, or $10 per thousand.

Portfolio: collection of investments of various types.

Power of attorney: a document authorizing a particular individual to act on behalf of the one signing the document. The signatures must be witnessed and notarized. For example, a broker who is granted limited power of attorney (or "discretion") may buy and sell securities in that account, but may not remove assets from the account.

Premium: for bonds, a premium refers to a price in excess of par value. For options, the premium is the dollar amount that a buyer pays or a seller receives for the option contract.

Pre-refunding: mechanism by which a bond issuer floats a new bond issue, the proceeds of which are used to pay off a pre-existing bond before its maturity date. The funds received from the second bond issue are invested in very safe investments, usually Treasury securities, that will mature on or about the time of the first call date of the first bond issue. When a bond is pre-refunded it almost always is assigned an AAA rating from the rating agencies due to the high quality of the investments in the escrow account established to redeem the bond at its call date.

Present value: today's value of a future payment or payments, discounted at a rate of interest. If you wish $2000 in 7 years and the rate of interest is 4 percent, you need to invest $1,520 today. Thus $1520 is the present value of $2000 in 7 years at 4 percent.

Primary market: the market for new securities issues (Initial public offerings, or IPOs). A market is primary if the issuer of the securities receives the funds from the securities which are sold. (See also, Secondary market.)

Prospectus: a formal offer describing securities that are to be sold on a primary basis. This offer must be filed with the Securities and Exchange Commission and must also be provided to potential purchasers of the security so that they may make informed decisions regarding the investment merits of the security. A preliminary prospectus is sometimes called a "red herring."

Put (or put option): for bonds, put is the bondholder's right to redeem the bond for a stated price before its final maturity. A put option is an option to sell the underlying security.

Qualified plan: a retirement plan that conforms to the rules established by the Internal Revenue Service. Funds accumulate on a tax-deferred basis until they are withdrawn. The employer makes contributions to the plan, which are eligible for certain tax benefits according to IRS rules.

Rating: the evaluation of investment and credit risk for a stock or bond or an insurance company.

Realized gain (or loss): the profit or loss that results when a securities transaction is completed. Realized gains result in taxable income. Realized losses may be used to reduce taxable income.

Risk: the measurable possibility of loss. (Unmeasurable risks are "uncertainty.") The greater the variability of returns of an investment, the greater the risk. Other types of risk include interest rate risk (if interest rates trend higher, the value of your bond portfolio declines) and purchasing power risk (inflation chews away at the value of your money).

Secondary market: the marketplace where most securities issues trade. When a security trades in the secondary market, the company that originally issues the security does not receive any proceeds from the transaction.

Settlement date: the date by which an executed order must be settled—when a buyer must pay for the securities purchased or a seller must deliver the securities. Usually the settlement date is five business days (excluding market holidays) from the trade date. Options and some Treasury securities settle on the next business day.

Share: a unit of ownership in a corporation.

Short position: occurs when a security is sold before it is purchased or when a sold security has not yet been delivered for settlement of a transaction. A security may be "sold short" with the hope of buying it back at a lower price (and a profit).

SIPC: The Securities Investor Protection Corporation. The main form of insurance for brokerage houses.

Split: when a corporation increases the outstanding shares of a security, it may do so in the form of a stock split. For example, a two-for-one split of a $50 stock would result in two shares of a $25 stock. A stock dividend is similar to a stock split from the investor's point of view. Neither a split nor a stock dividend will affect the investor's equity position in the company.

Spread: the difference between the bid and the offer price of a security. (See also, Bid and Offer.)

✓ **Standard & Poor's Corporation:** a rating agency that assesses the investment and credit risks of securities.

Stop order: an order to buy or sell securities at the prevailing market price as soon as a price threshold has been reached. May be a day or a good-until-cancelled order.

Stop price: See Stop order, above.

STRIPS: zero-coupon U.S. government bonds (See also, CATS.) The acronym STRIPS stands for Separate Trading of Registered Interest and Principal of Securities.

Tender offer: an offer made directly to shareowners to purchase or exchange securities. The offer may be made by the company itself or by outside individuals wishing to gain control of the company.

Ticker symbol: the "call letters" that identify a security for trading.

Trade date: the date on which a trade is executed.

Trading range: the price range between the highest and lowest prices of a security. Normally these prices are for the past fifty-two weeks.

Value Line Investment Survey: an investment advisory service that ranks stocks for "timeliness" and "safety." Value Line ranks stocks for performance over the next twelve months on a scale of 1 to 5, with 1 being the highest rank and 5 the lowest.

Volume: the total number of shares traded in a period, usually one day.

Window dressing: trading activity at the end of a quarter or at year-end that is done with the intent of improving the look of a portfolio. For example, a mutual fund manager may sell stocks that have declined or purchase stocks that have risen during the period so he or she will not be seen to have owned stocks that are losers.

Zero-coupon bonds: bonds sold at a deep discount to maturity value and make no periodic interest payments. (See also, Discount.)

ABOUT THE AUTHOR

NINA HILL is a registered representative and Certified Financial Planner® for a large brokerage firm. She graduated from the University of North Carolina at Chapel Hill with a degree in journalism and earned her Master of Business Administration degree from New York University, majoring in finance. She lives in New York City with her cat, Reece.